Rosh HaSh
Messianic Kingdom to Come

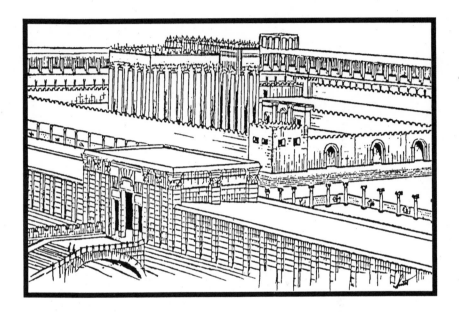

A Messianic Jewish Interpretation of the Feast of Trumpets

by Joseph Good

This book is dedicated in loving memory to my father, Joseph E. Good Sr., who I will soon see again in the Messianic Kingdom. The impact of his character and his walk with the L-rd will remain with me until then.

Acknowledgments

I wish to express my heart-felt thanks to:

Rose Good, my wife, who has prayed, supported, and advised me every step of the way.

Jo Herzberg, my hard working assistant, who selflessly donated her time and energy. She adopted this project as her own and was instrumental to its completion.

Mark Thompson and his wife **Betsy,** who opened the world of computer desktop publishing to us, enabling us to produce this and other works. Their suggestions as to style and formatting are seen on every page.

Kyle Ambrose, for being the English scholar that he is. Kyle provided a substantial amount of Biblical Research.

Asher Fowler, who assisted in the original Biblical research.

Andy Garza, who was a moving force in numerous all-night publishing and editing sessions.

Patty Greene, without whose help this book would not have been possible.

The members of Kehilat Tikvat Yisrael, who helped in countless ways.

Table of Contents

Rosh Hashanah and the Messianic Kingdom to Come

Foreword

As one begins a study of the Jewish festivals, a pattern portraying the redemption of G-d culminating in the Messianic Kingdom begins to surface in all areas of Judaic literature. In these various sources, the feast of Rosh HaShanah emerges as the threshold of the Messianic Kingdom. This book is a collection of scattered teachings on this festival that hopefully will restore to the body of Messiah these long forgotten truths. A composite of its doctrines, customs, and traditions define the eschatology of the Athid Lavo (the Coming Age).

For non-Jewish readers, the terminology may be foreign. Even for the Jew, some information may be new. These terms are used not to confuse, but rather to restore that which was seen and known in the first century C.E. (A.D.) It is hoped that this material will aid students of the scripture as they read the Gospels and the Epistles, which were written in the language of the festivals. In order to cause the reader to deal with the fact that the New Testament is a Jewish document, the names of books and persons in that portion of the scripture have been restored to their Hebraic form. The books and names of the First Covenant scriptures have been left in their familiar English form, because most people understand the Jewishness that is there. Hopefully, both segments of scripture will come alive and be seen as the complimentary portions that they are. In addition, numerous Rabbinical sources have been used. It is imperative that today's believers return to the ancient understandings that these writings present. Their validity is established as the scriptures take on new meaning and purpose. These writings, known as the Mishna, Midrashim, Talmud, Targumim, etc., will be new to many of the readers of this work. Their names and logic may be foreign at first, but the student who endeavors to learn will have a gold mine that is his from which to pull untold riches. It is strongly advised that each footnote, as well as note, be examined along with the text. It is hoped that the student will use the bibliography to further his or her understanding.

May the ancient understandings and ways be restored for the well-being of the believers in Yeshua the Messiah.

> Thus saith the L-rd, Let not the wise man glory in his wisdom, neither let the mighty man glory in his might, let not the rich man glory in his riches; but let him that glorieth glory in this, that he understandeth and knoweth Me, that I am the L-rd, which exercise lovingkindness, judgment, and righteousness in the earth; for in these things I delight, saith the L-rd.
> Jeremiah 9.23-24

PROLOGUE

Today, late in the twentieth century, living thousands of miles from the middle East, our perspectives of Bible times and doctrines are often perverted from their original meanings. The second coming of the Messiah Yeshua and the establishment of His earthly kingdom is a subject that is commonly written about. It is spoken of from pulpits across the nation, but seldom put in its original Jewish setting. This book is an attempt to do just that.

In the beginning, G-d created the earth as an abode for His throne. His creation was perfect in every way. Man was created by G-d in His image and given dominion over His creation. Within man was woman, and G-d separated her from man to be a helpmate and companion to him. Man was created with a free will, as he was created in the image of G-d, who has a free will. This free will had also been given to the angels. According to Ezekiel twenty-eight, Satan, known in Judaism as HaSatan, was created to worship G-d but perverted this worship by transferring the praise of G-d to himself. He led a rebellion of angels that joined with him in the sin of pride. This horde of angels turned-bad would become the demons confined to the earth. HaSatan set out to attack by suggestion and deceit the rightful rulers of the earth, Adam and Chava (Eve).

As Adam and Eve obeyed HaSatan within Gan Eden (the Garden of Eden), man lost his right to rule the planet. His power and glory were broken, and man was only a hollow shell of his former stature. The immortal had put on mortality, and the incorruptible had become corrupted. At this point G-d provided a plan of restoration. This restoration would come forth by a redeemer, in Hebrew, called a "go'el." The "go'el" was understood to be a man who would come from G-d, empowered by the Ruach haKodesh (the Holy Spirit) to defeat HaSatan, thereby redeeming man. G-d's law decreed that the man who sinned would die. In order to defeat the adversary, the "go'el" would have to be without sin and pay for the sins that man had committed. Because this man was empowered by the Ruach haKodesh, he was known as the "anointed one," which in Hebrew is the Maschiach (Messiah).

G-d's desire was for man to have faith that He through the Messiah would redeem man and restore him to his former position and greatness. The promise was that one day man would be returned to his immortality, and the earth would again be as Gan Eden. In order to teach man about the Coming One, and also to teach man the ways of G-d, the Jewish people were created. To this people, G-d gave His Torah (teaching and law), as well as the prophets who made fertile the plans of G-d. The faith in the redemption of G-d was defined within everything G-d gave to the Jewish people.

Four thousand years after the creation, the Messiah would come to the earth. He declared the basar (gospel) of the Malkut Shamayim (the Kingdom of Heaven), which was the expectation of all the people who looked for the redemption of G-d. This man named Yeshua, which means "Salvation," lived without sin, was falsely accused by jealous men, and died the death of a convicted criminal. His death was accepted by G-d as payment for the sins of mankind. Three days after His death, G-d raised Yeshua back to life by the Ruach haKodesh; but in His resurrection He had a new body, immortal and glorified. In Yeshua, the restoration is complete.

Fifty days after His resurrection, the Ruach haKodesh fell upon all who believed in Yeshua. They were anointed with power which tasted of the Olam Haba (the World to Come), which is promised following the total restoration of mankind. These first believers in Yeshua were all Jewish and remained Jewish in their life-style and faith. In Judaism, their faith was already centered in the message of Yeshua's redemption. For years the believers remained an active part of the Jewish community. Their synagogues, their worship, and their expectations were all Jewish.

With the salvation of Cornelius in Acts ten, to the surprise of the Jews, the basar (good news) of the kingdom was opened to Gentiles. Other Gentiles had become believers in the past, but had always become proselyte Jews. When the Gentiles became co-heirs of the Kingdom with the Jewish believers, major changes took place in the faith.

The gentile believers of the first century are seldom understood by today's Biblical scholars. They belonged to a group known as the "sebomenoi," or G-d- fearers. These were Gentiles who had left paganism and were already attending synagogues. They observed the Sabbath, as well as the Jewish festivals, and had incorporated into their own life-style many of the Jewish customs. Laws within the Torah defined how they were to be treated as well as how they were to live. It should be pointed out that observance of the Torah had nothing to do with the salvation of an individual, which could only be obtained by faith in the Messiah. For these "sebomenoi" believers, as well as the Jewish believers, the Torah defined their faith and their walk with G-d. Within the Sabbath, festivals, and customs, these two groups understood the working of the Messiah (Colossians 2.16-17). This Torah observance, however, was directly linked to an understanding of the doctrines of the faith.

Numerous problems were encountered for full fellowship to be established between these two groups which G-d had now joined together. Mainstream Judaism had a definite separation between these two groups, but now G-d used Rav Shaul (the

Apostle Paul) to address the situation among believers. His epistles, inspired by the Ruach haKodesh, repeatedly lay down guidelines to bridge this gap.

Faith in Yeshua was very widespread during the first century among the Jewish population, yet even more Gentiles were becoming believers. Proportionally, this greater number of Gentile believers eventually gave them an upper hand in decisions affecting most of the congregations outside of the region of ancient Israel. Events that happened in the one hundred years following the death of Rav Shaul changed the Faith to the point that today the Faith in Yeshua hardly resembles the Faith of the believers of the first century. Rav Shaul warned of this in his final address to the elders of Ephesus (Acts twenty), where he foretold that savage wolves would come in to destroy the faith.

The same year that Rav Shaul died (66 C.E.), the Jewish nation revolted against the Roman Empire. Four years later the Roman legions encircled Jerusalem at the feast of Pesach (Passover). Yeshua had warned the believers that the generation that was alive at the time of His death would see Jerusalem destroyed. He had instructed that when the city was circled by the enemy, they were to flee, which is what they did. Five months later the city fell. During this time, congregations in the Diaspora (dispersion) scattered throughout the Roman world, experienced radical changes. To support the Jewish people, or even Jewish customs, was interpreted as not being loyal to Rome. The greater numbers of Gentiles among the congregations began to make a difference as anti-Jewishness began to be popular.

In spite of this, Jews were still becoming believers, so much so that in 90 Common Era (C.E.), Rabbinical leaders who did not believe in Yeshua took steps to try to bar the Jewish believers from the synagogues. A benediction was added to the Amidah (a set of eighteen prayers recited daily by observant Jews) known as the Birkat haMinim. This benediction was a curse directed against the believers in Yeshua, with the idea that this would put an end to their rapid growth among the people. Still, more Jews accepted Yeshua as their Messiah. Now pressure was being put on the Jewish believers from three sides: first, from the non-believing pagans who hated anything Jewish; second, from the non-believing Jews who feared their power among the people; and third, within their own congregations by the new gentile believers who were entering into the faith already affected by rampant anti-semitism.

During 116 C.E. another war broke out in Egypt between the Jewish population and Rome. The Jewish population of Egypt was all but annihilated in this war, and again the position of the Jewish believers, as well as anything Jewish, was weakened within the congregations.

The final Jewish war occurred in 135 C.E. with the Bar Kochba rebellion. As the legions of Rome marched on the Jewish homeland, both believer and non-believer responded to the call to arms. The most prominent Rabbi of the time, Akiva, proclaimed that the leader of the Jewish forces was the messiah. With this declaration, the Jewish believers departed from the army for they could not serve another messiah. With their departure, the unbelieving Rabbis declared them "meshumed," which means traitors. This caused a separation of the Jewish believers from the Jewish community. Hadrian, the Roman Caesar, with vengeance came against the Jewish people and destroyed their army and nation. Throughout the empire anti-semitism was considered patriotism to Rome. All of this undermined the position of the Jewish believers and caused the congregations to turn from anything Jewish.

Toward the beginning of the fourth century C.E., Constantine became the Caesar of Rome. In his rise to power, he supposedly became a believer and joined the group now called Christians. In 325 C.E. he called the Council of Nicea, where he gathered the heads of the Christian community from throughout the empire. In this council, however, he purposely left out every Jewish leader. Laws were passed forbidding Jewish believers to circumcise their children, to observe the Jewish festivals or to rear their children as Jews. The Jewish believers were forced to cease being Jewish and to become, in every sense of the word, Gentiles. Pagan festivals such as Easter, lent, Christmas, and Sunday were substituted for the Biblical festivals of G-d. Not only were the Jewish believers gone for all practical purposes, but so were the "sebomenoi." The faith now was a totally different religion. Greek names, concepts, and religion became Christianity. The faith had been "gentilized."

Going back to the first century, the believers, both Jewish and "sebomenoi," understood the place of the Jewish festivals because of the gift of the Torah, which taught the doctrine. They understood that the Spring festivals taught on the Messiah's first coming and that the festivals of the fall taught on His return. They knew the teachings of the Rabbis that the Messianic Kingdom would begin on earth with the advent of Rosh haShanah. They understood the wedding of the Messiah, the coronation, the resurrection of the dead, as well as the beginning of the time of trouble.

CHAPTER 1

THE DUAL CONCEPT OF THE MESSIAH

Then said I (the Messiah), Lo, I come: in the volume of the book
it is written of Me.

Psalm 40.7

The volume of material contained in the scriptures and the
Jewish writings concerning the Messiah is unlimited. G-d not only
outlines the work Messiah will perform, but He also tells us many
details about Him (His lineage, birthplace, nature, etc.). History
records that in the period shortly before and for a brief time after
the first century C.E., Messianic expectation had reached its
greatest peak. The prophet Daniel, over four hundred years
before the time of Yeshua, had foretold that the Messiah would
appear in the midst of the fourth kingdom from the time of his
prophecy. The Messiah, according to Daniel seven, would then
establish His own kingdom that would be without end. From the
days of Daniel, four kingdoms had successively risen on the earth.
They were the Babylonian, Media-Persian, Greek, and Roman
Empires. In another prophecy, Daniel 9.24-27, Daniel had told
the time of the Messiah's coming as being approximately 400
years after the return of Nehemiah and Ezra. This expectation is
seen in Luke 3.15-16.

And as the people were in expectation, and all men mused in
their hearts of Yochanan (John), whether he were the Messiah,
or not; Yochanan answered, saying unto them all, I indeed
immerse you with water; but one mightier than I cometh, the
latchet of whose shoes I am not worthy to unloose: He shall

> immerse you with the Ruach haKadosh (the Holy Spirit) and with
> fire.
>
> Luke 3.15-16

By the time of Yochanan (John), the anticipation of the Messiah had generated a highly developed eschatological theology. This was expressed by numerous apocalyptic writings as well as the Targumim (Aramaic paraphrases of the scriptures) and orally transmitted rabbinic teachings. The exposition of scripture known as Midrash would tie together both obvious and obscure passages to present tangible doctrines of the Coming One. For thorough treatment of the eschatological doctrines of the first century, consult *Judaism in the First Centuries of the Christian Era / The Age of the Tannaim*, by George Foot Moore, Cambridge Harvard University Press; and *Palestinian Judaism in the Time of Jesus Christ*, by Joseph Bonsirven, S.J., Holt, Rinehart and Winston.

As the ancient Jewish scholars and Rabbis began to study the scriptural information about the Messiah, they encountered a serious problem: many of the passages seemed to contradict one another. Often the Messiah is seen as a conquering king, coming in judgment to establish a reign of peace on earth from Jerusalem, as in Zechariah Fourteen, Psalm Two, Isaiah 63-66, Jeremiah Twenty-three, for example. Other passages speak of a suffering servant who would come in humility, would be rejected and despised by His people, would die for the sins of men, and would then be resurrected by G-d: Isaiah Forty through Fifty-three, Sixty-one, Psalm Twenty-two, and Daniel Nine. From this paradoxical description of the Messiah came a First Century Common Era (A.D.) rabbinical teaching of two Messiahs.[1]

Most of the messianic passages of the Bible, as well as the

---

1) Mt. 11.2-3

majority of rabbinic commentary on the Messiah, are centered in the Conquering King. These passages present Him as a dynamic personality, who is anointed by G-d, not only to crush His enemies, but also to regather the dispersed of Israel and usher in her golden age. Diametrically opposed to this, another personality was also identified as the Messiah: lowly, humiliated, despised and persecuted.

This one, labeled the Suffering Servant by modern commentators, was anciently known as Messiah ben Joseph. His life ends in death, unlike His counter-part, the Messiah ben David (the ancient name for the Conquering King), who is immortal. An example of rabbinic commentary showing the Messiah ben Joseph and His death are found in Succah 52a, where the Gemara ask a question concerning the structure of the Temple having been altered as stated in the corresponding Mishnah.[2] This authority, according to the Gemara, came from Zechariah 12.12-14, where describing a period of mourning, says:

> And the land shall mourn, every family apart; the family of the house of David apart, and their wives apart; the family of the house of Nathan apart, and their wives apart; the family of the house of Levi apart, and their wives apart; the family of Shimei apart, and their wives apart; all the families that remain, every family apart, and their wives apart.
>
> Zechariah 12.12-14

Rabbi Dosa explained in this Gemara that the reason for the future mourning mentioned in the verse will be the slaying of the Messiah of the house of Joseph, the herald of the Messianic Age, who will precede the Messiah of the house of David.

A further development of the rabbinic doctrine of the Messiah ben Joseph (also known as Ephraim, who was the son of

---

2)   The Mishnah and the Gemara are the two respective portions of the Talmud.

Joseph) is found in Midrash Pesiqta Rabba 36. Here, the Messiah is being informed by G-d of what awaits Him on the earth:

> Their sins will be upon you like a yoke of iron. They will choke your spirit. Because of their sins, your tongue will cleave to the roof of your mouth. Do you accept this? If not, I will remove the decree from you.

> The Messiah replies: Master of the worlds, how long will this last?

> G-d replies: Ephraim, My true Messiah, ever since the six days of creation you have taken this ordeal upon yourself. At this moment, your pain is My pain.

> Messiah replies: Master of the worlds, I accept this with gladness in my soul, and joy in my heart, so that not a single one of the house of Israel should perish. Not only for those alive, but also the dead. It is enough that the servant be like the Master.
> Midrash Pesiqta Rabbah 36

Evidence from the gospels showing that the suffering servant was identified with the Messiah is found in Luke 24.13-35. In this passage Yeshua, on the day of His resurrection is found in journey with two men traveling to Emmaus. The two travelers with Yeshua, despondent over His death, but not having realized His resurrection, are suddenly rebuked by Yeshua as He says:

> The he said unto them, O fools, and slow of heart to believe all that the prophets have spoken: ought not Messiah to have suffered these things and to enter into His glory?
> Luke 24.25-26

This statement by Yeshua shows that the people interpreted the suffering servant passages as pertaining to the Messiah, as well as those of the conquering king, indicating their belief in two separate Messiahs.

This anticipation of two Messiahs by the Jewish people of the first century is the background for the question posed by Yochanan the Immerser (John the Baptist) to Yeshua as to whether He was the Messiah (indicating one, singular), or if they were to expect another. Many well-meaning people have incorrectly assumed and taught that Yochanan was going through a time of doubt. The truth is that Yochanan knew Yeshua was the Messiah, for G-d had told him so,[3] and he himself had already been used by G-d to identify Yeshua as the Messiah.[4] His question was specifically whether Yeshua would fulfill all of the prophecies concerning Messiah, or whether the Rabbis, who said there would be two Messiahs, were right. Yeshua's answer[5] is a paraphrase of various passages that Rabbis identified as referring partially to Messiah Ben Joseph and partially to Messiah Ben David.[6] Therefore, Yeshua was expressing, in dramatic language that was clear to His listeners, that He would fulfill all of the Messianic prophecies. Rather than send two Messiahs with two different roles, G-d would send one Messiah in two separate appearances or comings. Messiah's first coming fulfilled the prophecies of the Suffering Servant, while the second coming will fulfill those of the Conquering King.

Often the prophecies concerning the second coming of the Messiah, in which He is seen as the Conquering King, are told in combination with prophecies of His first coming as the Suffering

---

3) Mt.3.13; Mk.1.9-11; Lk. 1.39-41; 3.21-22

4) Jn. 1.19-36; Jn. 3.23-26

5) Mt. 11.4-6

6) Rabbi Redak; Shorasim (a Rabbinic commentary); Rabbi A.J. Rosenberg, ed., The Book of Isaiah. (New York: Judaica Press, 1982) Vol.2, pg. 544

Servant. Sometimes there is not a clear distinction between the two comings, and it is only through the unfolding of history that we are able to separate the two. Traditionally, the prophecies have been studied by taking a chapter here and there and applying it to either the first or second coming. The bulk of scripture, especially within the Tanach (the Hebrew Bible), is usually not dealt with. Vast areas of scripture from this type of exegesis will only produce Jewish history.

It is important to keep in mind that the Messiah was supposed to perform His role in two different missions on earth. The significance of it to the festivals is that G-d divided them into two groups, and it shall be demonstrated in another section how the two groups of festivals relate to the first and second comings of the Messiah. Specifically, this book concerns Rosh haShanah, the festival of Messiah's kingship, his judgment of the world, and his wedding.

CHAPTER 2

THE CHOSEN PEOPLE

In order to understand the festival of Rosh haShanah in the framework of the Jewish festivals, the calling of Israel must be dealt with. This is a subject that many have difficulty with, for calling the Jewish people "The Chosen People" sounds like arrogance. What it means is that Israel has a job to do. G-d commissioned Israel to perform a particular task.[1] He does not love Israel more than other nations; His love is universal. But just as G-d calls each person to play a specific role in his life, He calls nations to play a particular role in history. Three questions will be answered in this section: Where did the Jewish people come from? What were they called to do? and Has that task changed?

A little over three thousand, five hundred years ago G-d called Abram out of Ur of the Chaldees, a region steeped in paganism, to walk with Him in the land of Canaan.[2] G-d promised Abram the land of Canaan and descendants too numerous to count. G-d changed his name (Abram means "Exalted Father") to Abraham ("Father of Nations"). He gave him a son, Yitzchak

---

1) Deut. 4.1-8; 7.1-11; Isa. 41.8-9; 44.21; Mt. 5.13-16

2) Gen. 12.1-9

(Isaac),[3] and a grandson, Ya'acov (Jacob).[4] G-d gave Jacob the same promise He had made to Abraham.[5] Because G-d appeared to him at that time, Jacob named the meeting place Peniel--"Face of G-d." At the same time, G-d changed Jacob's name (meaning "Supplanter") to Yisrael (meaning "A Prince with G-d").[6] Yisrael (Israel) had twelve sons, the founders of twelve tribes.[7] It was their descendants whom G-d established as the nation of Israel at Mount Sinai. There He gave them their government, laws, customs, and moral code. G-d was the author of the laws of Israel, not Moses, nor any other man. The other nations of the world chose their own kings and developed their own customs, but Israel was different. G-d Himself chose these things for Israel, because He chose Israel to be a light to the other nations,[8] by which they might see, know, and desire G-d for themselves.

> Now therefore hearken, O Israel, unto the statutes and unto the judgments, which I teach you, for to do them, that ye may live, and go in and possess the land which the L-rd G-d of your fathers giveth you. Ye shall not add unto the word which I command you, neither shall ye diminish aught from it, that ye may keep the commandments of the L-rd your God which I command you. Keep therefore and do them; for this is your wisdom and your understanding in the sight of the nations, which shall hear all these statutes, and say, Surely this great nation is a wise and understanding people. For what nation is there so great, who hath G-d so nigh unto them, as the L-rd our G-d is in all things

---

3) Gen. 17.19

4) Gen. 25.24-28

5) Gen. 28.10-22

6) Gen. 32.24-32

7) Gen. 29.31-30.24; 35.16-18

8) Deut. 7.1-11; Isa. 41.8-9; 44.21; Mt. 5.13-16

that we call upon him for? And what nation is there so great, that
hath statutes and judgments so righteous as all this law, which I
set before you this day?
Deuteronomy 4.1,2, 6-8

Rav Shaul (the Apostle Paul), in his letter to the Messianic
believers in Rome, reaffirmed this commission of G-d given to
the Jewish nation:

What advantage then hath the Jew? or what profit is there of
circumcision? Much every way: chiefly, because that unto them
were committed the oracles of G-d.
Romans 3.1,2

I say the truth in Messiah, I lie not, my conscience also bearing
me witness in the Ruach haKodesh (the Holy Spirit), that I have
great heaviness and continual sorrow in my heart. For I could
wish that myself were accursed from Messiah for my brethren,
my kinsmen according to the flesh: who are Israelites, to whom
pertaineth the adoption, and the glory, and the covenants, and
the giving of the Law, and the service of G-d, and the promises;
Whose are the fathers, and of whom, as concerning the flesh
Messiah came, Who is over all, G-d blessed for ever. Amen.
Romans 9.1-5

These passages tell us the things G-d gave to Israel: the
oracles of G-d, the adoption, the glory, the covenants, the Law,
the service of the Temple, the promises, the fathers, and most
importantly the Messiah. He gave Israel their manner of dress,
their diet, their celebrations, their music, and their holidays. Why
did He give them? He wanted to set Israel apart and make them
a testimony of Himself to the other nations.[9]

It was to a Jewish audience that Yeshua the Messiah
delivered the well-known "Sermon on the Mount."[10] In that

9) ibid

10) Mt.5.1-7.29

message, Yeshua spoke of the Jewish people and how G-d had chosen them to reveal His redemption and His Messiah through the Torah and their lifestyle:

> Ye (Israel) are the salt of the earth: but if the salt have lost his savior, wherewith shall it be salted? it is thenceforth good for nothing, but to be cast out, and to be trodden under foot of men. Ye are the light of the world. A city that is set on an hill cannot be hid. Neither do men light a candle, and put it under a bushel, but on a candlestick; and it giveth light unto all that are in the house. Let your light so shine before men, that they may see your good works, and glorify your Father which is in heaven.
> Mattatiyahu (Matthew) 5.13-16

The following passage has often been used by misinformed people to condemn the dietary laws, the Sabbath, and the festivals. The truth is that it tells us they were given to teach on the Messiah, His work, and His glory.

> Let no man therfore judge you in meat, or in drink, or in respect of an holyday, or of the new moon, or of the sabbath days: Which are a shadow of things to come; but the body is of Messiah.
> Colossians 2.16-17

There is the example of Rav Shaul, who spoke of himself in the present tense as an Israelite,[11] and a Pharisee.[12] He celebrated the festivals[13] and made offerings in the Temple.[14] All of this was long after the death and resurrection of Yeshua and after he himself was a believer.

Rav Shaul (the apostle Paul) has generally been treated by

11) Rom. 11.1

12) Acts 23.6

13) Acts 28.21

14) Acts 21.26; 24.17-18

Christian commentators as having departed from Judaism upon receiving Yeshua as his Messiah. This erroneous teaching has done more to harm the doctrines of faith in Yeshua than possibly any other single factor in the last two thousand years. It is not consistent with the Bible or with the historical record of the early believers in Yeshua.

The primary passage that establishes that Rav Shaul was himself a Torah-observant Jew years after receiving Yeshua is found in Acts twenty-one. The setting for the passage is where Rav Shaul went up to Jerusalem to keep the feast of Shavuot (Pentecost) along with a party from the various congregations of Asia Minor. This party would consist of believers that are both Jewish as well as Gentile.

> And when we were come to Jerusalem, the brethren received us gladly, and the day following Rav Shaul went in with us unto Ya'acov (James); and all the elders were present. And when he had saluted them, he declared particularly what things G-d had wrought among the Gentiles by his ministry. and when they heard it, they glorified the L-rd, and said unto him, Thou seest, brother, how many thousands of Jews there are which believe; and they are all zealous of the Torah (law): and they are informed of thee, that thou teachest all the Jews which are among the Gentiles to forsake Moses, saying that they ought not to circumcise their children, neither to walk after the customs.
> Acts 21.17-21

Notice that the charge is that Rav Shaul is teaching the Jewish believers in the diaspora to cease being Torah-observant, as well as not to walk after the customs of the Jews. From the context of the passage, it is evident that Ya'acov (James) and the other elders [Shimon (Peter), Yochanan (John), et cetera] are determined to prove to this body of Jewish believers that Rav Shaul has not departed from being a Torah-observant Jew, nor was he teaching other Jews to do so. Somehow, over the centuries,

Christianity overlooked this passage, teaching that Rav Shaul ceased to follow the teachings of Moses and the customs of the fathers. From this misunderstanding, Christian teaching has become unbalanced concerning the writings of Rav Shaul. Unfortunately, this misinterpretation has caused a great amount of confusion and wrong doctrine to influence Christianity.

> What is it therefore? The multitude must needs come together: for they will hear that thou art come. Do therefore this that we say to thee: We have four men which have a vow on them; them take, and purify thyself with them, and be at charges with them, that they may shave their heads:
>
> Acts 21.22-24a

The vow that is spoken of is the Nazarite vow spoken of in Numbers 6. The phrase "be at charges with them" refers to purchasing the necessary sacrifices listed in Numbers 6 and mentioned in Acts 21.26. According to Acts 18.18, Rav Shaul himself had also taken a Nazarite vow. Thus, two questions arise: "Why were Jewish believers offering animal sacrifice when Yeshua was the final sacrifice?" and "Why were James and the other elders endorsing the sacrifices?" The answer to both of these questions is found in Hebrews 10.4. The passage relates that it is not possible for the blood of bulls and goats to take away sins. This was true before the time of Yeshua and remains true today. If animal sacrifice was never for the removal of sins, what purpose, then, did it serve? G-d's wisdom had ordained that man should understand the mission of the Messiah. Consequently, G-d had given the gift of the various Temple rites[15] to the Jewish people. Within these rites would be five different types of sacrifices: 1) burnt offering, 2) guilt offering, 3) sin offering, 4) peace offering, and 5) bread offering. Each one of these would teach different aspects concerning the Messiah. Yeshua, being the final sacrifice,

---

15) Rom. 9.4

refers to the fact that only His sacrifice is acceptable to G-d for our sins. The offering of these sacrifices by the Jewish believers and their endorsement by James and the other elders in no way compromised the truth that salvation is by faith and not by the keeping of the commandments.

> And all may know that those things, whereof they were informed concerning thee, are nothing; but that thou thyself also walkest orderly, and keepest the Torah.
> Acts 21.24b

Instead of James' rebuking the thousands of Jews who believe and are zealous for the Torah, Rav Shaul is asked to prove to them that he is also a Torah observant man. It is important to know that this event occurred approximately twenty-nine years following the resurrection of Yeshua. Further evidence is seen throughout the book of Acts. He consistently attends the synagogue in each of the communities that he visits. In Acts 20.6 he keeps Hag ha Matzah (the festival of unleavened bread) and then conducts a Havdolah service (concluding service for the Sabbath, inaugurating the first day of the week) as described in Acts 20.7-12. In Acts 24.11,17, Rav Shaul tells the Roman Governor that he had come to Jerusalem for the festival of Shavuot, to worship G-d, and to bring offerings (Temple sacrifices) and alms. According to Acts 23.6, Rav Shaul spoke of himself as a Pharisee, and finally in Acts 28.17, he professed to the Jewish leaders in Rome that he had committed nothing against his people or the customs of the fathers.

Two important factors have caused us to misconstrue not only the teachings of Rav Shaul, but also today's concepts of the law and anything that is considered to be Jewish. The first of these is a misunderstanding of the book of Galatians. To the casual reader that has failed to research the background, the book appears to condemn Judaism, and to emphatically proclaim that believers have been set free from the Torah (law). If this were true, Rav Shaul would be in sin to continue his own life following the commandments of Moses.

Until Acts ten, everyone that was a believer was either Jewish by birth or had become a proselyte. Following the salvation of Cornelius who was a G-d-fearer (Gentiles who attended synagogue and adhered to certain points of Jewish observance but were not considered Jewish), the belief that only Jews could be saved had to be altered, acknowledging that Gentiles had also been made co- heirs of the kingdom.[16] It was never doubted that Jewish believers should continue in their observance of the Torah. It must not be understood that observance of any commandments would gain either salvation or righteousness with G-d. Those are attained by faith, whereas the commandments deal with life-style and obedience to a commission from G-d. However, during the first century C.E., certain Jewish believers were trying to convince the Gentile believers that after having received Yeshua as their Messiah by faith, they must then also keep all the commandments in order to be righteous with G- d. In other words, they were requiring the new Gentile believers to become Jewish. This is Judaizing. Rav Shaul's letter to the congregation in Galatia is a rebuttal against the teachings of these Jewish believers. It should be noted that the majority of the Jewish believers did not follow this practice of Judaizing. It should also be pointed out that the faith in the Messiah is a Jewish faith[17] and that the Gentiles within the faith did participate in many of the things that G-d had given to the Jews. For a better understanding of the Gentile participation in the faith, a study of the G-d-fearers is suggested.

---

16) Ephesians 3.1-7

17) Romans eleven.

The second factor that has affected our out-of-balance theology today is the course of events that took place for the next two and a half centuries following Rav Shaul's death. A far larger number of Gentiles were coming into the faith than Jews. Often, they would bring pagan concepts and religious practices with them. Shortly after the death of Rav Shaul (66 C.E.), the Jewish people rebelled against the Roman Empire and made a bid for independence (66-70 C.E.). At that point anything considered Jewish was interpreted as unpatriotic to Rome. Anti-semitism was popular. To make matters worse, a second war with Rome (135 C.E.), again weakened the role of the Jewish believers in the Messianic congregations. As the Jewish voice died, the anti-semitic Gentiles ripped out every trace of the Jewish people that could be found. Substitution of Biblical festivals by pagan beliefs was rampant. By the time of the Council of Nicea (325 C.E.), Constantine, who was very anti-Semitic, had taken over the church. Laws were issued forbidding Jewish believers to circumcise their children, Pesach was replaced with Easter (the Babylonian fertility goddess), Sukkot was replaced by Christmas (the Roman birthday of the sun god), and so on. Even the Gospels and the Epistles were gentilized when they were translated into other languages and were given common Gentile names and idiomatic thoughts, causing people to miss the intended Jewishness of those scriptures.

In conclusion, Rav Shaul never departed from being a Jew but rather continued in the life-style and commandments that G-d had given to his people. His walk was in liberty, accurately portraying the doctrines of the Messiah through that life-style. As long as the Temple stood, he and the other Jewish believers continued to participate in its services. The congregations that they formed were actually Messianic synagogues comprised of both Jewish and non-Jewish believers. Its structure, holidays, and message were all Jewish. Tragically, our spiritual adversary robbed us of the blueprints of our faith that so accurately showed us Yeshua the Messiah.

He wrote to the congregation at Corinth (both Jews and non-Jews):

> Therefore let us keep the feast, not with old leaven, neither with the leaven of malice and wickedness; but with the unleavened bread of sincerity and truth.
> I Corinthians 5.8

Obviously, the believers in the First Century kept the festivals or this statement could not have been made. Why did they keep them? There are two reasons: to learn about the Messiah and to teach about the Messiah. This is the calling of Israel, especially of those Jewish people who know the Messiah. This is why the study of Rosh haShanah is necessary. In the festivals G-d explains, defines, demonstrates, and reinforces Himself and His plan.

CHAPTER 3

THE FESTIVALS

And the L-rd spake unto Moses, saying, "Speak unto the children of Israel, and say unto them, Concerning the feasts of the L-rd, which ye shall proclaim to be holy convocations, even these are my feasts."

Leviticus 23:1-2

Like all of Biblical Judaism, the festivals (feasts) in some way teach us about the Messiah. Leviticus twenty-three is one of the key chapters for unlocking the entire Bible. If one can obtain a good working knowledge of the festivals, then he will have in his possession G-d's blueprint for mankind.

The festivals are multi-faceted. Some speak of historical events such as Israel's departure from Egypt, while others look forward to the future redemption through the Messiah at the end of days. All have ties to agriculture. Many have highly developed Temple rituals,[1] while others are primarily home ceremonies.[2]

The seven festivals are celebrated in two different seasons, which correspond to the two agricultural seasons. The four spring festivals take us from the beginning to the ingathering of the barley harvest. The three fall festivals begin at the time of the ingathering of wheat and other crops. Naturally, these harvest seasons depend upon rain. In Israel there is a time of rain in the spring (former rain) and a time of rain in the fall (latter rain). This

---

1) Pesach, Firstfruits of the Barley Harvest, Shavuot, Yom Kippur, and Sukkot

2) Hag HaMatzah, and Sukkot

division relates to the two appearances that Messiah is to make on the earth:

> ...and he shall come unto us as the rain, as the latter and former rain unto the earth.
>
> Hosea 6.3c [3]

The Spring Festivals -- The Former Rain

The spring festivals are known as historical festivals, because they commemorate events in Israel's past, namely the slaying of the lamb, the Exodus from Egypt, the crossing of the Red Sea, and the receiving of the Torah. The work of the Messiah Yeshua during His first coming is seen most clearly in these festivals.

Pesach

The first feast is on the fourteenth day of the first month (Aviv or Nisan), and is called Pesach (Passover).[4] It commemorates the time when the children of Israel were slaves in Egypt. Israel cried out to G-d in their affliction, and G-d raised up a deliverer--Moses.[5] Moses demanded that Pharaoh let G-d's people go a three-day journey into the wilderness to hold a feast

---

3) Joel 2.23; James 5.7-8

4) Ex. 12.1-7

5) Ex. 3.1-4.17

and make sacrifice to G-d.[6] Pharaoh refused. G-d gave Moses the authority to call down plagues on the land of Egypt.[7] After the first nine plagues, Pharaoh would still not let the people of Israel go.[8] Finally, G-d said that on the tenth day of the month of Aviv, each household should take a male lamb, one year old (mature but young), without spot or blemish.[9] The household was to keep its lamb for four days, during which time they were to inspect him and to make sure that he was perfect.[10]

On the fourteenth at three o'clock in the afternoon (the twain of the evening),[11] the father gathered his family to the doorway. According to Exodus 12.6, the lamb was to be killed at a specific time.

> And ye shall keep it up until the fourteenth day of the same month: and the whole assembly of the congregation of Israel shall kill it in the evening.
> Exodus 12.6

"In the evening" in Hebrew would be said: "bain haarbayim" (literally translated "between the evenings"). This phrase suggests the time, a point between the sun's declining in the west and its setting, (approximately 3:00 p.m.). Within the Temple, the day was divided into quarters. The quarter between 12:00 noon and 3:00 p.m. was called the minor evening oblation, while that between 3:00 p.m. and 6:00 p.m. was called the major evening oblation. Therefore, "between the evenings" means between

---

6) Ex. 3.18; 5.3; 8.27

7) Ex. 4.17; 7.1-10.23

8) Ex. 10.24-29

9) Ex. 12.3-5

10) Ex. 12.3-4

11) Ex. 12.6

those two periods, or 3:00 p.m. The hours were counted from daylight (approximately 6:00 a.m.) till sundown (approximately 6:00 p.m.). The ninth hour when Yeshua was slain would therefore be 3:00 p.m., the same time the lamb had been slain in Egypt.

In the doorway the father lay his hand on the lamb, thereby identifying with him symbolically. The laying on of hands in Hebrew is called "Semicha" and is referred to in Hebrews six as being one of the elementary doctrines of the faith in Yeshua.

> Therefore leaving the principles of the doctrine of Messiah, let us go on unto perfection; not laying again the foundation of repentance from dead works, and of faith toward G-d, of the doctrine of immersions, and of laying on of hands, and of resurrection of the dead, and of eternal judgment. And this we will do, if G-d permit.
> Hebrews 6.1-3

According to Roland de Vaux in his book, *Ancient Israel, vol. 2*, pg. 416, the laying on of hands is done on the head of the animal to be sacrificed. This animal must meet all the scriptural qualifications. The action is not seen as a magical gesture establishing contact between G-d and man, nor does it symbolically imply that the victim is a substitute for the man. Instead, it is a solemn attestation that this sacrifice has come from this particular man who is performing the "semicha" upon the animal's head. He declares that the sacrifice, which is going to be presented to G-d, is offered in his name, and that the fruits of the sacrifice shall be his.

The father cuts the throat of the lamb, and applies its blood to the lintel and to each sidepost around the door.[12] The mother roasts the lamb[13] on a pomegranate stick over an open fire,[14] and prepares a special meal.[15] At sundown (approximately six p.m.), the day changed (the Jewish day goes from sundown to sundown, i.e., six p.m. to six p.m.)[16] to the fifteenth of Aviv.

That night, the fifteenth, the Jewish people in Egypt ate the lamb with bitter herbs and matzah (unleavened bread) according to the commandment G-d had given.[17] One was to eat with his staff in his hand, and his sandals on his feet.[18] The people were forbidden to go outside their houses,[19] for that night an angel of death was coming to Egypt.[20] He would slay the firstborn sons in every house, whether Egyptian or Jewish, royal or slave, human or animal.[21] But G-d made a promise to the people within those houses which had the blood of the lamb on their doorposts. G-d himself would hover over those houses to protect them from the

---

12) Ex. 12.7

13) Ex. 12.8-9

14) Ex. 12.7; Pesachim 7.1

15) Ex. 12.8

16) Gen. 1.5

17) Ex. 12.8

18) Ex.12.11

19) Ex.12.22

20) Ex. 12.12,23,29

21) Ex. 12.29

The Festivals

angel of death.[22] This is where the name Pesach (Passover) came from. That night Pharaoh told Moses to take the children of Israel and to go as Moses had said (for a three-day journey).[23]

Several points of importance revolve around the fact that the children of Israel were only going into the wilderness for three days. The children of Israel were owned by Pharaoh, and not Egypt.[24] With the death of Pharaoh,[25] his ownership over them would cease; therefore, freeing them to continue to the promised land. Understanding that the children of Israel left Egypt on the 15th of Aviv,[26] only being granted a three day leave,[27] Pharaoh could not have approached their camp any later than the evening of the seventeenth of Aviv. That this approach was in the evening is established by Ex. 14.20-21. In reconstructing the probable chronology of these days, note that the children of Israel begin the Exodus during the night[28] between the hours of midnight and dawn. The first leg of their journey carries them to Sukkot.

---

22) Ex. 12.23

23) Ex. 12.31

24) Gen. 47.13,26

25) Psa. 136.15; Psa 74.13,14, (Leviathan is a term the Rabbis identified with Pharaoh)

26) Num. 33.3

27) Ex.12.31

28) Ex. 12.29-37

Apparently, from the context of Ex. 13.19-20, the purpose of travelling to Sukkot was to secure the body of Joseph. The people pitch their tents there[29] as Moses retrieves the coffin, possibly between the hours of sunrise and noon, still the 15th of Aviv. The journey of the 15th continues on to Etham,[30] where the people camp for the night, now the 16th. On the morning of the 16th, the children of Israel journey to Pi Hahiroth next to the sea.[31] It is here in the evening, now the 17th, that Pharaoh approaches the Hebrew camp,[32] being held at bay through most of the night as the camp of Israel crosses the sea.[33] Pharaoh and his army enter the sea during the morning watch,[34] where G-d slays them.[35] Therefore, the children of Israel emerge alive from the depth of the sea before sunrise on the morning of the 17th. According to the calculations of the Rabbanan,[36] the Exodus from Egypt began on a Friday (15th), which would therefore cause the crossing of the sea to be on a Sunday, (17th).

It has already been established that the pesach in Egypt had been slain on the 14th of Aviv (which in that year was a Thursday), had left Egypt, having visited the grave of Joseph, on the 15th, (Friday), and had crossed the sea on the 17th, (Sunday). It should be no surprise that Yeshua's death, burial, and resurrection would

---

29) Num. 33.5

30) Num. 33.6

31) Num. 33.7

32) Ex.14.9

33) Ex. 14.19-22

34) Ex.14.23-24; the morning watch is the last third of the night just before dawn

35) Ex.14.25-31

36) The Biblical and Historical Background of the Jewish Holy Days, by Abraham P. Block, KTAV Publishing, pg. 186

not only parallel the dates but also the days of the week. Traditional misunderstanding that Yeshua was slain on a Friday stems from the following verse.

The Jews therefore, because it was the Preparation, that the bodies should not remain upon the cross on the Sabbath day, (for that Sabbath day was an high day,) besought Pilate that their legs might be broken, and that they might be taken away.
Yochanan (John) 19.31

An interesting parallel is that Yeshua is placed in the tomb of Joseph of Ramah (Arimathea in Greek). Ramah, the city of Joseph, means "seat of idolatry" in Hebrew. As noted, Moses had also gone to the tomb of another Joseph on the 15th, to retrieve Joseph's body; thereby leaving his tomb empty. Joseph of Egypt, the seat of idolatry, had been an excellent picture of the coming Messiah by all that had happened in his life: he was hated by his brothers, cast into a pit, sold as a slave, falsely accused, committed to the dungeon; but, through the spirit of G-d, raised to be ruler of Egypt second only to Pharaoh. He was sent by G-d to preserve life, during the famine of death. In later years, he revealed himself to his brothers, who all this time had thought him to be the ruler of the Gentiles, rather than one of their own brethren. Even though he holds the power of death in his hand for the sins of his brothers, he extends mercy and forgiveness. His very name means "G-d Will Add," showing that there is another coming after him. This is fulfilled in his brother Benjamin, which means "Son of My Right Hand." Yeshua's first coming proclaimed the promise of His second coming, and He is the Son of the Right Hand.

Hag haMatzah

The second spring festival commemorates the events of the night of the fifteenth of Aviv--the meal of the lamb with unleavened bread and bitter herbs--and the actual departure from Egypt. It is called Hag Ha Matzah (Festival of Unleavened Bread), because during this week-long feast the children of Israel have been commanded to eat matzah (unleavened bread).

Firstfruits of the Barley Harvest

The third festival falls during the week of Hag Ha Matzah on the day after the weekly Sabbath (Saturday)--in other words, the first Sunday after the fifteenth of Aviv.

During the first century C.E., the date of the Firstfruits of the Barley Harvest was a hotly contested issue. The Pharisees maintained that the proper date would be the 16th of Aviv, also called Nisan, while the Sadducees endorsed the Sunday following the weekly Sabbath during Hag haMatzah (the Festival of Unleavened Bread). The debate was centered in the wording of Leviticus twenty-three.

> And the L-rd spake unto Moses, saying, Speak unto the children of Israel, and say unto them, When ye be come into the land which I give unto you, and shall reap the harvest thereof, then ye shall bring a sheaf of the firstfruits of your harvest unto the priest: and he shall wave the sheaf before the L-rd, to be accepted for you: on the morrow after the sabbath the priest shall wave it.
> Leviticus 23.9-11

On the surface it would seem to be an obvious conclusion that the Sadducees were right, for everyone knows that the day following the Sabbath is Sunday. However, the issue is complicated by the fact that during the week of Hag haMatzah there are two sabbaths. During the Jewish year there are seven sabbaths known as "Shabbaton" or "high sabbaths." These sabbaths fall upon particular calendar days rather than on days of the week. The 15th of Aviv is the first shabbaton during the Jewish year. It is the first day of Hag haMatzah and the sabbath that the

Pharisees felt that Leviticus 23.11 spoke of. Besides the substantiation that Yeshua rose from the dead on a Sunday, and He is called "the firstfruits of those that rise from the dead,"[37] it can be established from Leviticus twenty-three that the Sadducees were correct.

> And ye shall count unto you from the morrow after the sabbath, from the day that ye brought the sheaf of the wave offering; seven sabbaths shall be complete: even unto the morrow after the seventh sabbath shall ye number fifty days; and ye shall offer a new meat offering to the L-rd.
> Leviticus 23.15-16

The only way that it could be guaranteed there would be both seven sabbaths and fifty days is to use the calculations of the Sadducees.

Historically, this was the day that Israel went down into the depth of the Red Sea but emerged alive on the other side, for G-d parted the waters before them.[38] The pagan Egyptians also entered the cleft in the waters to destroy Israel, but G-d caused the waters to return to their normal state, thereby killing Pharaoh and his soldiers.[39] The death of Pharaoh ended his rights to ownership of the children of Israel.

According to Genesis 47.13-26, Pharaoh owned all the people in Egypt except for the Egyptian priests. Naturally, this would include the slaves of Egypt. In order for the children of Israel to go to the promised land, they would have to be set free from this ownership. Moses, following G-d's instruction, had only requested of Pharaoh that the people be allowed to go three

---

37) I Corinthians 15.20-23

38) Ex.14.21-22, 29

39) Ex. 14.23-28; Ex. 15.19; Psa. 136.15

The Festivals

days'journey into the wilderness to hold a festival to G-d. Pharaoh transgressed his own commandment of telling the people to go by pursuing the people; therefore, he was responsible for his own death. If he had but waited till the end of three days, Moses would have returned with the people, for G-d cannot lie. With his death in the midst of the sea, Egypt no longer had claim on the sons of Israel, and they were free to go on to the Promised Land.

In Leviticus twenty-three this day is called B'Yom Haneefchem Et Ha Omer, "The Day You Bring in the Sheaf of the Wave Offering." G-d commanded the people, once they got to the Promised Land, to bring the firstfruits of their barley harvest as a wave offering[40] before Him on this day.[41]

Counting of the Omer -- Journey to Mount Sinai

From the Red Sea, Israel traveled forty-seven days until they reached the mountain of G-d. This date would be given to them as their fourth festival.[42]

This chart shows the forty-seven days of the journey to Mount Sinai plus the three days of separation to fulfill the fifty days between the crossing of the sea and the giving of the Torah. Remember that Yeshua's resurrection and the falling of the Ruach haKodesh (the Holy Spirit) will parallel this same time period.

---

40) Lev. 23.11

41) Lev.23.10

42) Lev. 23.16-22

Aviv (Nisan)

Sun	Mon	Tue	Wed	Thu	Fri	Sat
17	18	19	20	22	22	23
24	25	26	27	28	29	30

Zif (Iyar)

Sun	Mon	Tue	Wed	Thu	Fri	Sat
1	2	3	4	5	6	7
8	9	10	11	12	13	14
15	16	17	18	19	20	21
22	23	24	25	26	27	28
29	30					

Sivan

Sun	Mon	Tue	Wed	Thu	Fri	Sat
		1	2	3	4	5
6						

As established before, the children of Israel left Egypt on Friday the 15th of Aviv, crossed the sea on Sunday the 17th, and then journeyed for forty-seven days to Mount Sinai. Today's modern Jewish calendar only gives twenty-nine days for the month of Iyar (the ancient Zif). However, such imminent scholars as the late Yigdal Yadin (known as the dean of Israeli archeologists) believed that possibly other calendars were in use in the earlier times. As late as the first century C.E., the Qumran sect was using a solar calendar with twelve months of thirty days each, with an intercalary day at the end of every three months. This is the calendar used in the above chart.

Shavuot

G-d instructed Moses to tell the people to purify themselves for three days.[43] On the fiftieth day after coming up alive out of the sea, they were to approach the mountain. That day was thereafter known as the Revelation of G-d at Mt. Sinai,[44] where He appeared on the mountain. A shofar (trumpet made from a ram's horn) sounded louder and louder.[45] Fire was seen on the mountain. The wind roared, and the ground shook. While Israel stood in awe, the voice of G-d brought forth the Torah.[46] According to Jewish tradition, He spoke not only in Hebrew, but in every known tongue at that time as well.

Rabbi Joseph Hertz, in his *Authorized Daily Prayer Book* on p. 791 states, "The Revelation at Sinai, it was taught, was given in desert territory, which belongs to no one nation exclusively; and it was heard not by Israel alone, but by the inhabitants of all the earth. The Divine Voice divided itself into the seventy tongues then spoken on earth, so that all the children of men might understand its world-embracing and man-redeeming message."

When G-d gave the Torah on Sinai, He displayed untold marvels to Israel with His voice. What happened? G-d spoke and the Voice reverberated throughout the world. ...It says, And all the people witnessed the thunderings (Exo. 18.15). Note that it does not say "the thunder," but "the thunderings"; wherefore, R. Johanan said that G-d's voice, as it was uttered, split up into seventy voices, in seventy languages, so that all the nations

---

43) Ex. 19.10-15

44) Hertz, Dr. Joseph, The Authorized Daily Prayer Book, (New York: Block Publishing Co.), pg. 790

45) Ex. 19.19

46) Ex. 20.1-17

should understand. When each nation heard the Voice in their own vernacular, their souls departed [i.e. they were in fear], save Israel, who heard but who were not hurt...

Exodus Rabbah 5.9

On the occasion of matan Torah (the giving of the Torah), the Bnai Yisrael (the children of Israel) not only heard Hashem's (the L-rd's) Voice but actually saw the sound waves as they emerged from Hashem's (the L- rd's) mouth. They visualized them as a fiery substance. Each commandment that left Hashem's (the L-rd's) mouth traveled around the entire Camp and then came back to every Jew individually, asking him, "Do you accept upon yourself this Commandment with all halachot (Jewish law) pertaining to it?" Every Jew answered, "Yes," after each Commandment. Finally, the fiery substance which they saw, engraved itself on the luchot (tablets).

The Midrash Says on Shemot; Rabbi Moshe Weissman, Benei Yakov Publications (1980) pg. 182.

The fourth festival commemorates the awesome events that took place at Mt. Sinai. It is called Shavuot or the Feast of Weeks (Pentecost), for the children of Israel are to count seven weeks from the festival of Firstfruits, and then observe the following day as Shavuot. These forty-nine days are called,"The Counting of the Omer."[47] They connect the festival of Firstfruits (of the barley harvest) to Shavuot (the beginning of the wheat harvest). Since the Firstfruits festival falls on the day after the Sabbath, Shavuot will also.

Shavuot was designated by the rabbis as the Atzeret (a festive gathering for the conclusion of a festive season, a concluding feast) of Pesach. In the Targum Onkelos, Numbers 28.16 designates Shavuot in this way. For a complete listing of the Rabbinic passages on Shavuot as the Atzeret to Pesach, see: *A Dictionary of the Targumim, the Talmud Babli and Yerushalmi,*

47) Lev. 23.9-16

and the Midrashic Literature, compiled by Marcus Jastrow, The Judaica Press, Inc., page 1103. As Pesach was the beginning of the barley harvest, with the waving of the sheaf on the following Sunday, each day was thereafter counted until Shavuot, making a natural bridge between the two festivals. In addition to the agricultural aspect, there was also the historical link with the journey from Egypt to Mount Sinai. With Yeshua's resurrection, a third thread stitches together Pesach and Shavuot as He instructs the disciples to remain in Jerusalem until they have had power poured out on them from on high.[48] It is at Shavuot that this is fulfilled,[49] completing a work that He had begun at Pesach. An excellent article on this is found in *The Biblical and Historical Background of the Jewish Holy Days* by Abraham P. Bloch, KTAV Publishing House, Inc., page 179-182.

Not only do the four spring festivals have a historical and agricultural significance, but they are also prophetic of future events. A term in Hebrew for festival, or feast, is mo'ed, and it means a "set time," or an "appointed time."[50] G-d has appointed seasons during the year that He would require the men of Israel to be present in Jerusalem.[51] Notice that they are called the appointments of the L-rd, given to Israel to observe.[52] The implication here is that G-d has an appointment to perform something with Israel on these dates. Another word used in connection with the festivals is mikrah, which is translated as

---

48) Luke 24.49

49) Acts two

50) Lev. 23.4

51) Deut. sixteen

52) Psa. 81.3; II Chron. 8.13; Lev. 23.2,4,37,44

"convocation" in most Bibles.[53] It literally means "rehearsal" or "recital." The implication of this is that the festivals are times that Israel rehearses various aspects of the plan of G-d. This is good preparation for the times that the L-rd fulfills the appointments. As the pilgrims traveled year by year to Jerusalem for these festivals, the Rabbis taught and speculated on the Messianic aspects of these appointments and rehearsals.

One thousand, five hundred years after the time of Moses in the land of Judea, a prophet named Yochanan the Immerser (John the Baptist) was drawing large crowds as he spoke. One day, Yochanan boldly pointed to a man approaching his crowd and said, "Behold the Lamb of G-d, which taketh away the sin of the world." (Yochanan 1:29) This man was like no other man that ever lived, for He was Yeshua, the Messiah of Israel.

For three and one-half years Yeshua traveled throughout the land of Israel, healing the blind and the lame, cleansing lepers, healing the deaf, raising the dead to life, and preaching the good news.

In English, the words "good news" and "gospel" are synonymous. In Hebrew, the term is "basar," while in Greek it is "euangelion." Since the fall of Adam, G-d had promised to restore man to the dominion and stature that he once had held. Adam had been created in the image of G-d. His environment was perfect; and if sin had not caused his fall, he would still be alive today. Man, driven from the garden following the fall, became only a diminutive of what he had been. The earth also had changed, for G-d had placed a curse upon it. Man's future was bleak with the exception of a hope seen in the prophesies of a Coming One who would conquer sin, defeat death, and bring about the restoration of both man and earth. Prophets, kings, and

---

53) Lev. 23.2

priests had all spoken of this man and event. This became known as the "basar" or "good news." It was well defined in the Jewish mind long before Yeshua walked upon the earth. As Adam had been a king over the earth under the rule of G-d, so the redeemer to come would also be a king. The Kingdom of Heaven, or "Malkut Shamayim," in Hebrew, would come to earth in this king. The kingdom was to be a time of physical as well as spiritual resurrection; therefore, healing, miracles, and divine manifestations of the power of G-d were expected. Yeshua's work in His first coming fulfilled only part of the promised restoration. This restoration will be completed in His second coming.

During the last week of His life, on the tenth of Aviv, He sat upon the Mount of Olives east of Jerusalem and wept over the city:

> And when he was come near, he beheld the city, and wept over it, saying, If thou hadst known, even thou, at least in this thy day, the things which belong unto thy peace! but now they are hid from thine eyes. For the days shall come upon thee, that thine enemies shall cast a trench about thee, and compass thee round, and keep thee in on every side, and shall lay thee even with the ground, and thy children within thee; and they shall not leave in thee one stone upon another; because thou knewest not the time of thy visitation.
> Luke 19.41-44

This particular day had been earmarked for one and one-half millennia by G-d for special happenings. The tenth of Aviv is the same day that in Egypt each household of Israel had taken a perfect male lamb without spot or blemish into their house.[54]

In Exodus 12.2, G-d had required that a lamb be taken to each household on the tenth of Aviv. In fulfillment of this, the Messiah

---

54) Ex. 12.3

entered the city Himself on the tenth of Aviv. In Yochanan (John) 12.1, Yeshua comes to Bethany.

> Then Yeshua six days before the Passover came to Bethany, where Lazarus was which had been dead, whom He raised from the dead.
>
> Yochanan (John) 12.1

Throughout the book of Yochanan, the "Passover" refers not to the fourteenth (the actual day of the Passover) but rather to the entire eight days of Passover and Hag haMatzah. Since the first day of Hag haMatzah, the fifteenth, is a Shabbaton (High Sabbath) this is generally considered the beginning of the Feast. The Jewish historian, Josephus, also called the fifteenth the first day of Pesach.

In the chart below, counting back six days before the fifteenth of Aviv, Yeshua must have arrived at the house of Lazarus on the ninth of the month. That night, which will be the tenth, a supper is prepared for Yeshua. This is probably the traditional meal concluding the Sabbath and inaugurating a new week. The following day, which is still the tenth, Yeshua enters the city and goes to the Temple, just as the lamb had been taken into the house in the Egyptian Pesach.

> On the next day much people that were come to the feast, when they heard that Yeshua was coming to Jerusalem, took branches of palm trees, and went forth to meet Him, and cried, Hosanna, Blessed is the King of Israel that cometh in the name of the L-rd.
>
> Yochanan (John) 12.12-13

Nisan (Aviv)

Sun	Mon	Tues	Wed	Thur	Fri	Sat
					1	2
3	4	5	6	7	8	9
10	11	12	13	14	15	16
17						

On this day Yeshua looked down from the Mount of Olives, where there was a great procession of priests, musicians, singers, dancers and throngs of people heading from the east to Jerusalem and the Temple.[55] They had the lamb that would be slain in the public sacrifice on the fourteenth. This lamb stood in the Temple for four days for all to see that he was indeed without spot.[56] As they entered the city, the crowds waved palm branches before the lamb and sang Psalm 118. As they entered the Temple area, they waved the branches to the six directions (north, south, east, west, up, and down) as they recited: "Ana Adonai Hoshia-na, Ana Adonai Hoshia-na. Ana Adonai Hatzlicha-na, Ana Adonai Hatzlicha-na. Baruch Ha Ba B'Shem Adonai," which means the following:

Oh L-rd, please save us, Oh L-rd, please save us. Oh L-rd, send us prosperity, Oh L-rd, send us prosperity. Blessed is He that comes in the name of the L-rd.

Yeshua descended the Mount of Olives, and followed the same route down which the lamb had just been led. The same

55) Lk. 19. 41-44

56) Lk. 19.45-22.6; Jn. 12.12-50; Mk. 11.1-13.37; Mt. 21.1-26

crowds who waved the palm branches before the Pesach lamb met the Lamb of G-d who would take away their sins, and cried out:

"Hosha-na Baruch ha Ba B'Shem Adonai B'rucha Malchut David Avinu ha Ba-a B'Shem Adonai Hosha-na Ba-m'romim"

and

"Baruch Ha-Melech ha-Ba b'Shem Adonai Shalom ba-Shamayim v'Chavod Ba-M'romim," which means the following:

"Hosanna--Save us. Blessed is He that comes in the name of the L-rd! Blessed is the kingdom of our father David that comes in the name of the L-rd. Hosanna in the Highest!"

"Blessed is the King that comes in the name of the L-rd Peace in Heaven and Glory in the Highest"

Even as the Passover lamb stood for four days tethered in the Temple in public view, so Yeshua sat and taught in the Temple courtyard for all to examine. During this time, the Sadducees,[57] the Pharisees,[58] and others asked Yeshua their hardest questions. Their purpose was to find fault in Him, but they could not. Indeed, He was without spot and blemish.

On the morning of the 14th at the third hour (9:00 a.m.), the lamb in the temple was bound to the altar.[59] At the same time outside the city walls, Yeshua was both tied and nailed to the tree.[60] For six hours both the lamb and Yeshua awaited death. At

---

57) Mt. 22.23-33; Mk. 12.18-27; Lk. 20.27-38

58) Mt.22.15-22; Mk. 12.13-17; Lk. 20. 19-26

59) Psa. 118.27

60) Mk. 15.25

the ninth hour (3:00 p.m.), the High Priest ascended the altar in the Temple, took his knife, and killed the lamb, pronouncing the words, "It is finished." This is the term that the priest in the Temple would say with the conclusion of the daily peace offering as well as the various special festival offerings.

At exactly the same moment, Yeshua on the tree gave up His spirit with the same words and died.[61] The death of Yeshua, occurring simultaneously with that of the lamb in the Temple, was no accident. The slaying of the Passover lamb was a rehearsal of the sacrifice of the Messiah. Rav Shaul (the Apostle Paul), in his letter to the believers in Corinth, referred to the Messiah as the Passover.

> For even Messiah, our Passover (Lamb), is sacrificed for us.
> I Corinthians 5:7b

The magnitude of what is happening here cannot be realized until the transcendence of the Messiah is acknowledged.

> In the beginning was the Word, and the Word was with G-d, and the Word was G-d. The same was in the beginning with G-d. All things were made by him; and without him was not any thing made that was made. In him was life; and the life was the light of men. And the Word was made flesh, and dwelt among us, (and we beheld His glory, the glory as of the only begotten of the Father,) full of grace and truth.
> John 1.1-4,14

The One who hung on the tree kept the mo'ed, the time appointed 1500 years before, to the exact minute. Even as the ancient Pesach lamb had delivered the people from the plague of

---

61) Jn. 19.30

death and from slavery by his blood, so the Messiah provided salvation through the shedding of His blood.

Yeshua died at three o'clock in the evening. They hurried to place Him in the grave by sunset,[62] at which time the next festival--Unleavened Bread--begins.[63] The first day of that festival is the day that the children of Israel ate the Pesach lamb with matzah and bitter herbs. [64] During the meal, a ceremony was rehearsed in which a piece of matzah is broken, wrapped in linen, and buried.

This ceremony, called "afikoman," dates back to the days of Yeshua. During the first part of the "seder" (the Pesach meal), a piece of matzah is removed from a special bag and broken. This bag contains three portions of matzah and is know as the "unity bag." The ceremony of breaking the middle matzah is called "yachatz" which means "to break." Half of the broken matzah is placed back in the bag, while the other half is wrapped in linen and buried. Later, the children who watched where the broken matzah was buried, try to steal it and hold it for ransom from their father. The seder cannot continue until the father retrieves this matzah, now known as the "afikoman." During the days of the Temple, the afikoman came after the dinner, but was not the last thing that the participants ate, because that was required to be the Pesach lamb itself. However, in any seder that was conducted outside the city of Jerusalem, the afikoman would be the last thing eaten during the entire night, because the Pesach lamb was only allowed to be slain in Jerusalem. In this event, the afikoman became a substitute for the lamb itself. After the destruction of the Temple in 70 C.E., the afikoman universally became the last

---

62) Jn. 19.31-42

63) Lev. 23.6; Ex. 13.3-10

64) Ex. 12.8-10

thing eaten at the seder, always representing the Pesach lamb. The word afikoman is believed to come from a Greek word meaning "that which comes after." In Yochanan (John) 6.51 during Pesach in the Galilee, Yeshua said,

> I am the living bread which came down from heaven: if any man eat of this bread, he shall live forever: and the bread that I will give is my flesh, which I will give for the life of the world.
> Yochanan (John) 6.51

It is important to note that His statement takes place in the Galilee, for there it would be known that the afikoman is a symbol of the Pesach lamb. Therefore, His references to "eating His flesh" should be understood in its counterpart -- the afikoman. The term, "broken," refers to His body being destroyed, but not to His bones breaking, for this would have disqualified Him from being a Pesach sacrifice.

> For these things were done, that the scripture should be fulfilled, A bone of him shall not be broken.
> Yochanan (John) 19.36

Like the matzah Yeshua's body was broken, wrapped in linen cloths,[65] and placed in the grave,[66] thereby keeping the appointment.

---

65) Jn. 19.40

66) Jn.19.41-42

The children of Israel traveled three days into the wilderness. All hope was lost as the Egyptians cornered them at the Red Sea.[67] Death was imminent, but G-d opened a way of salvation through the midst of the dark sea.[68] Israel in faith went down into the dreadful sea and climbed its banks alive on the other side--a resurrected people. In parallel, the Messiah lay in the grave for three days,[69] and on the 17th of Aviv, He came up alive, never to die again.[70] That year the 17th of Aviv fell on the first day of the week;[71] therefore, it was the feast of Firstfruits. [72] It was the beginning of the barley harvest, thus reminding us of newness of life. Just as grain springs to life from a cold, dead seed, so Messiah Yeshua became the firstfruits of those who will rise from the dead.

But now is Messiah risen from the dead, and become the First Fruits of them that slept. For since by man came death, by man came also the resurrection of the dead. For as in Adam all die, even so in Messiah shall all be made alive. But every man in his own order: Messiah the First Fruits; afterward they that are Messiah's at His coming.
I Corinthians 15:20-23

On the day of His resurrection, Yeshua told His disciples what He would fulfill at His next appointment (mo'ed).

And He said unto them, These are the words which I spake unto you, while I was yet with you, that all things must be fulfilled,

---

67) Ex. 14.8-12

68) Ex. 14.21-22, 29-30

69) Mt. 12.40

70) Rev. 1.18

71) Jn. 20.1; Lk. 24.1; Mk. 16.1-2; Mt. 28.1

72) Lev. 23.11

which were written in the Torah of Moses, and in the Nevi'im (Prophets), and in the Tehilim (Psalms), concerning Me. Then opened He their understanding, that they might understand the Scriptures, And said unto them, Thus it is written, and thus it behooved Messiah to suffer, and to rise from the dead the third day: And that repentance and remission of sins should be preached in His name among all nations, beginning at Jerusalem. And ye are witnesses of these things. And, behold, I send the promise of My Father upon you: but tarry ye in the city of Jerusalem, until ye be endued with power from on high.

Luke 24.44-49

At His ascension forty days after the resurrection, He again told of the power that His believers would receive to be His witnesses.

And, being assembled together with them, commanded them that they should not depart from Jerusalem, but wait for the promise of the Father, which, saith He, ye have heard of Me. For Yochanan truly immersed with water, but ye shall be immersed with the Ruach HaKodesh (Holy Spirit) not many days hence. But ye shall receive power, after that the Ruach HaKodesh (Holy Spirit) is come upon you: and ye shall be witnesses unto Me both in Jerusalem, and in all Judea, and in Samaria, and unto the uttermost part of the earth.

Acts 1.4,5,8

Remember that from the day of the Firstfruits of the Barley Harvest, the people of Israel counted the forty-nine days before the festival of Shavuot. As the disciples of Yeshua were awaiting the promise He spoke of, they were also counting the days and anticipating the next festival. Meanwhile, the Rabbis and scribes were reminding the people of the historical events connected with the festival, that is, the dramatic revelation of G-d at Mt. Sinai. Now, 1,500 years later, G-d kept His appointment to reveal Himself, through a group of people that He empowered to be witnesses. What was perceived anciently on the mountain (the fire, the wind, tongues)[73] would now be observed in the believers.

And when the Day of Shavuot was fully come, they were all with one accord in one place. And suddenly there came a sound from heaven as of a rushing mighty wind, and it filled all the house where they were sitting. And there appeared unto them cloven tongues like as of fire, and it sat upon each of them. And they were all filled with the Ruach HaKodesh and began to speak with other tongues, as the Ruach gave them utterance.
Acts 2.1-4

This concludes the four festivals that occur in spring, the time of the former rain, paralleling Messiah's first coming. Just as Pesach was the appointment for the death of the Messiah, Hag Ha Matzah for His burial, Firstfruits for His resurrection, and Shavuot for the revelation of G-d through believers, so also will Yom Teruah (The Feast of Trumpets), Yom Kippur (The Day of Atonement), and Sukkot (The Feast of Tabernacles) be important appointments in the plan of G-d. As the spring festivals were fulfilled literally to the day, as each taught important principles in the plan of G-d, and as they fell in a natural chronological progression compatible with the scriptural plan of G-d, so we can expect the fall festivals to do also.

The Fall Festivals -- The Latter Rain

The fall festivals take place in the seventh month, Tishri, which is the time of the latter rain. As it was observed how precisely the spring festivals taught the first coming of the Messiah, it can, likewise, be seen that His second coming is contained in the fall festivals.

---

73) Ex. 20.18; Exodus Rabbah 5.9

Yom Teruah -- Rosh Hashanah

Yom Teruah, the Feast of Trumpets, is also called Rosh haShanah (literally "Head of the Year"), the Jewish New Year. It teaches about the coronation and wedding of the Messiah, the rewards of the court, the oseif (gathering of the nobles), the Day of judgment, beginning of the Messianic kingdom, Jacob's Trouble, the resurrection of the dead, Teshuvah, and the birthday of the world. These themes will be developed individually by chapter later in this book.

Yom Kippur

Yom Kippur, the Day of Atonement, is considered the holiest day in the Jewish year. In the days of the Temple, there was an elaborate ritual involving two goats, one to be slain and one to be led off into the wilderness, symbolically bearing away the people's sins. The blood of the slain goat was borne by the high priest into the Holy of Holies. There this blood was sprinkled before the mercy seat of G-d. This was the only day of the year that the inner portion of the Temple could be entered and only by the high priest. At this time he came "face to face" with G-d. On this day G-d grants or denies atonement for the coming year. For this reason Yom Kippur would forever be known as Yom HaPeduth, Day of Redemption. As each year there was a temporal atonement and redemption, the Scriptures speak of a prophetic Day that Messiah will have returned, and the redemption will have been completed.[74]

Even as in this yearly ritual, the high priest would sprinkle

---

74) Isa. 59.20-21; Zech. 14.1- 15; Rev. 19.11-16

the assembled people for their cleansing, so will Messiah in His second coming do likewise.[75] The appointment communicated by this festival is the literal, physical second coming of the Messiah to the earth. With the Messiah's second coming on Yom Kippur, there will be another day of judgment of those who have survived the seven years of trouble (tribulation). For this reason, this day is also known as Yom haDin (the Day of judgment). It is on Yom Kippur that the Shofar haGadol (the Great Shofar) is blown to gather in the surviving believers from the awesome days. The interval between Rosh haShanah and Yom Kippur is known as Yamin Nora'im (the Days of Awe).

Sukkot

Sukkot, the Feast of Tabernacles or Booths, commemorates the time when Israel traveled in the wilderness as G-d led them. They lived in booths--temporary dwellings called sukkot in Hebrew. During this time G-d lived with the people in His own Tabernacle, the Mishkan. He also provided a cloud of covering that shaded the people by day and warmed them by night. G-d provided food[76] and water[77] for the people. G-d commanded the families of Israel to live in temporary shelters annually for the week of this festival.[78] In the Temple a magnificent ceremony took place in which the people rejoiced during the pouring of water and wine over the altar.[79] The major prophetic themes are

---

75) Isa. 52. 13-15, Targum Yonathan ben Uzziel on Isa 52.13; Mt. 24.27- 35

76) Ex. 16; Num. 11.31-35

77) Ex. 17.1-7

78) Lev. 23.42-43

79) Jn. 7.37-39

the Messianic Kingdom, the birth of the Messiah,[80] the dedication of the Temple, the pouring out of the living water, and the future protection of Israel in the wilderness.

As each festival approached, the entire nation was thrown into preparation. The elders of each village sent work crews to repair roads and bridges and to prepare for the thousands of pilgrims soon to flood toward the capital. The rabbis began approximately a month before the festival to teach not only the historical, but also the agricultural aspects of the festival. Each festival was full of various ceremonies and customs. The rabbis took each ceremony, custom, historical fact, et cetera, and coordinated symbolic and related passages of scripture into each facet of the festival. Even obscure references would often become major understandings associated with a particular festival. An example of this is the water pouring ceremony on Sukkot.

This ceremony, known as the Beit Hashoevah (the House of the Waterpouring), was conducted daily during the festival. At the time of the special Sukkot offerings, the priests assigned to perform this function set about slaughtering the sacrifices. A second group of priests went out the Eastern Gate of the Temple to the Valley of the Motza. There they cut willow trees at least twenty-five feet in length. The priests then aligned themselves shoulder to shoulder in several rows approximately thirty feet apart. At a signal, they each stepped forward on the right foot, swinging the willow branches to the left in unison. As they stepped forward on the left foot, the willows were swung to the right. Thus they proceeded toward the city. The waving of the willow branches produced the effect of a rushing wind (Ruach or spirit) approaching the Temple. Meanwhile, the Cohain haGadol (the High Priest) and his assistant had left the Temple from the Water

---

80) See Appendix I

Gate and gone to the Pool Shiloah (Siloam) and retrieved a vase of water known as Mayim Hayim (Living Water). This water was placed into a golden vessel while the assistant priest held a silver vessel full of wine. As the priests in the Valley of Motza started back to the Temple, so did the group at Shiloah. As each party approached their respective gates, a shofar was blown, and then a single flute began to play. The priests with the sacrifices ascended the altar, placing the animals on the fire. Those with the willows circled the altar seven times, then lay their willows against the base of the altar, forming a sukkah over its top. The High Priest and assistant also ascended the altar pouring out the water and wine. As this was done, the people sang Isaiah 12.3.

> Therefore with joy shall you draw water out of the wells of salvation (Yeshua).
>
> Isaiah 12.3

It was probably at this time, during Sukkot, that the Messiah Yeshua cried out the following:

> In the last day, that great day of the feast, Yeshua stood and cried, saying, If any man thirst, let him come unto me, and drink. He that believeth on me, as the scripture hath said, out of his belly shall flow rivers of living water.
>
> Yochanan (John) 7.37-38

Before the festival, the Rabbis taught every passage within the scriptures dealing with the pouring of water, living water, et cetera. It is the day following Sukkot that Yeshua is found in the women's court of the Temple. This day is also a festival know as Shemini Atzeret (the Eighth Day). Shemini Atzeret today is followed the next day by another festival known as Simchat Torah (Rejoicing in the Torah). However, in the days of the Temple, Shemini Atzeret and Simchat Torah were celebrated on the same day. It is in this setting that those teachers who rejected Yeshua bring the woman caught in adultery before Him to hear His judgment regarding her. Just the day before, these same men had participated in the Sukkot water pouring ceremonies and had heard Yeshua cry out that if any man thirsted, to come to Him and He would give them a drink of living water.[81] Being teachers, they had taught any related passages, as expressed before. With this understanding, what Yeshua did by writing in the earth takes on new meaning, for these Rabbis would have known and taught the passage from Jeremiah 17.12-13.

> A glorious high throne from the beginning is the place of our sanctuary. O L-rd, the hope of Israel, all that forsake thee shall be ashamed, and they that depart from me shall be written in the earth, because they have forsaken the L-rd, the fountain of living waters.
>
> Jeremiah 17.12-13

When Yeshua wrote in the earth (probably their names), He fulfilled an obscure scriptural reference already associated by these same rabbis with the water pouring ceremony. The fact that they had just rejected Yeshua's cry concerning the living water must have stung deeply. It is interesting to note that He was questioned about the Torah on the day known as "Rejoicing in the Torah."

Sukkot was also known as the "feast of Dedication," for it was at this feast that Solomon concluded the dedication of the first Temple.

A custom of placing four great lights in the midst of the Temple during the festival gave it the name of "feast of lights." The day following Sukkot is known as Shimini Atzeret and is attached to the festival. It was on this day that Yeshua declared in the midst of these lights that He was the Light of the world.

---

81) Jn. 7.37-39

As the festival of Sukkot is often referred to as the "Season of Our Joy," it is understandable why this is the appointed time for Yeshua's birth. It is interesting to note that when the Messiah was born, angels appeared to shepherds of Bethlehem declaring the message of the Messiah's birth which echoes the ancient liturgy of Sukkot.

> And the angel said unto them, Fear not: for, behold, I bring you good tidings of great joy, which shall be to all people. For unto you is born this day in the city of David a Savior. . .
>
> Luke 2.10-11

For more evidence on Yeshua's birth occurring during the festival of Sukkot, see Appendix I.

To keep G-d's commandments and appointed festivals was cause for jubilation. The rejoicing of Sukkot is seen in these quotes from the Mishnah.

> Devout men and men of (good) deeds would dance before them with the flaming torches [that were] in their hands and would utter before them words of songs and praises; and the Levites with harps, lyres, cymbals, trumpets, and countless musical instruments (stood) on the fifteen steps that descend from the Court of the Israelites to the Women's Court - corresponding to the fifteen Songs of Ascent in Psalms. . .
>
> Sukkah 5.4

> They said, 'Whoever did not see the rejoicing of Beit HaSho'evah, never saw rejoicing in his lifetime.'
>
> Sukkah 5.1

This rejoicing ties the festival into its prophetic emphasis of being the feast that portrays the Messianic Kingdom. During the festival, seventy sacrifices were offered with each being understood as a representation of one of the seventy nations of the world. Unlike the other six festivals which center on Israel alone, this festival portrays the time that G-d will rule over the world.

And the L-rd shall be king over all the earth: in that day shall there be one L-rd, and his name one.

Zechariah 14.9

In the Messianic Kingdom, all the nations of the world will come to Jerusalem yearly for the keeping of the festival.

And it shall come to pass, that every one that is left of all the nations which came against Jerusalem shall even go up from year to year to worship the King, the L-rd of hosts, and to keep the feast of Sukkot. And it shall be, that whoso will not come up of all the families of the earth unto Jerusalem to worship the King, the L-rd of hosts, even upon them shall be no rain. And if the family of Egypt go not up and come not, that have no rain; there shall be the plague, wherewith the L-rd will smite the heathen that come not up to keep the feast of Sukkot. This shall be the punishment of Egypt, and the punishment of all nations that come not up to keep the feast of Sukkot.

Zechariah 14.16-19

Conclusion

As stated before, all of the festivals play a historical, typical, and prophetic role. Each of the seven Biblical festivals contribute to the overall plan of G-d of the restoration of man and the earth. The next appointment to be kept is that of Rosh haShanah, where G-d will inaugurate His kingdom upon earth.

The Two Calendars

CHAPTER 4

THE TWO CALENDARS

Biblically, the Jewish people have two calendars. Actually there are four calendars according to Jewish tradition as evidenced by this Mishnah:

> There are four New Years. On the first of Nisan is the New Year for Kings and for Festivals (religious); on the first of Elul is the New Year for the tithe of animals -- R. Eliezer and R. Simon say, On the first of Tishri -- on the first of Tishri is the New Year for the years, for Sabbatical Years, for Jubilee Years, for planting and for vegetables (civil); and on the first of Shevat is the New Year for Trees, according to the view of the School of Shammai, but the School of Hillel say, On the fifteenth thereof.
> Rosh haShanah 1.1

For the purposes of this book, only the religious and civil calendars are used. The religious calendar starts in the spring with the month Aviv or Nisan (about March or April). This is the calendar that is used in Leviticus twenty-three. The civil calendar begins in the fall with the month of Tishri or Ethanim[1] (about September or October). Therefore, there are two New Years: Aviv 1 in the religious year and Tishri 1 in the civil year. This concept of two calendars is very important in a study of the Jewish festivals. At one time, Abraham and his descendants had only one calendar, the one we call the civil calendar, beginning in Tishri. In fact, this was the only calendar in use until G-d commanded the first Pesach lamb to be slain in Egypt.

---

1) I Kings 8.2

Even though both calendars (civil and religious) are in use throughout the scriptures and continue to the present, only the religious calendar is used to compute dates following its institution in Exodus twelve. Therefore, when it is read in Genesis 8.4 that Noah's ark rested upon Mount Ararat on the seventeenth day of the seventh month, it is understood to be the month of Aviv, which is the seventh month on the civil calendar. However, when reading II Chronicles 29.2-20, the seventeenth day of the first month (when Hezekiah enters the Temple to make sacrifice after it has been cleansed) should also be understood as Aviv, which is the first month on the religious calendar. It is of interest that these two events occur on the same day that Yeshua rises from the dead.

There is an interesting spiritual application to the two calendars. The earth had a physical birthday (Tishri 1), and then Israel had a spiritual birthday (Aviv 1). Those who believe in the Messiah (the Pesach lamb) experience a new beginning of their days. In this new calendar (that does not take away their physical birthday), the believer will have new dates different from that of the world.

A by-product of creation was the establishment of time. This is what is meant by "in the beginning."

In the beginning (of time) G-d created the heaven and the earth. And the earth was without form, and void; and darkness was upon the face of the deep. And the Spirit of G-d moved upon the face of the waters. And G-d said, Let there be light: and there was light. And G-d saw the light, that it was good: and G-d divided the light from the darkness. And G-d called the light Day, and the darkness He called Night. And the evening and the morning were the first day.
Genesis 1.1-5

That day was Tishri 1 -- the birthday of the world, the

beginning of creation. Consequently, Adam was created on Tishri 6, and the first Sabbath was Tishri 7.

In a Biblical Jewish year, there were twelve months of thirty days' length, making a total Biblical year of three hundred and sixty days.

This can be computed by examining Genesis 7 and 8. In this passage on Noah's flood, the waters rise on the earth for one hundred and fifty days.[2] Note that the rain began to fall on the seventeenth day of the second month, Bul,[3] and then is abated as the ark rests upon Mount Ararat on the seventeenth day of the seventh month, Aviv.[4] Obviously, there are thirty days in each month, as five months are spoken of in the passage, equalling one hundred and fifty days.

By the first century C.E., there were several calendars being used.[5] The calendar that was generally in use at the time of Yeshua was one employing the use of witnesses that had seen the testimony of the New Moon. The Sanhedrin, being convinced that the New Moon was present, then declared the beginning of the month. Therefore, there was not a set pattern to each month as there is today. Some of the months then, as now, were only twenty-nine days while others were thirty. About every third year, an extra month was added as a leap month called Ve-Adar.

Today there are 354 days in a Jewish year, with a corrective month occurring seven times every nineteen years. The present

---

2) Gen. 7.24

3) Gen. 7.11

4) Gen. 8.4-5

5) Block, Abraham, Historical Background of the Jewish Holidays (New York: KTAV Publishing Co.,1978) pg. 186-187

calendar, instituted by Hillel II in 360 C.E., obviously post-dated Yeshua by several hundred years.

The Civil Calendar

1. Tishri (Ethanim)	7. Nisan (Aviv)
2. Cheshvan (Bul)	8. Iyar (Zif)
3. Kislev	9. Sivan
4. Tevet	10. Tammuz
5. Sh'vat	11. Av
6. Adar	12. Elul

That G-d did not take away the civil calendar when giving the religious is established by the following passages which identify Tishri as the agricultural new year.[6]

> ...and the feast of ingathering (Sukkot), which is in the end of the year, when thou hast gathered in thy labours out of the field.
> Exodus 23.16b

> And thou shalt observe the feast of weeks (Shavuot), of the firstfruits of wheat harvest, and the feast of ingathering (Sukkot) at the year's end
> Exodus 34.22

> Here is an interesting reference to the month Tishri (also called Ethanim): "...in the month of Ethanim...that is, the seventh month. 'In the month that the ancient ones called the first month but now it is called the seventh month.'"
> Targum Yonathan ben Uzziel on I Kings 8.21

---

6) Deut. 14.22-29; 15.1-18

The Targumim are ancient paraphrased translations of the scriptures into Aramaic. Until recently, most scholarship held the view that Aramaic replaced Hebrew as the vernacular, following the return of the Babylonian captivity (539 B.C.E.). Now, many scholars believe that both languages were in common use. In the liturgical services, the scriptures were read in Hebrew followed by a recitation of the Targum covering the same portion of scripture. Far from simple translations, the Targumim were virtual commentaries, reflecting many of the religious ideas of the time. The two best known Targumim are those of Onkelos on the Torah and that of Yonathan ben Uzziel (Jonathan) on the Prophets.

As mentioned, in Exodus twelve G-d changed the calendar, or rather added an additional calendar:

> And the L-rd spake unto Moses and Aaron in the land of Egypt, saying, "This month (Aviv or Nisan) shall be unto you the beginning of months: it shall be the first month of the year to you.
> Exodus 12:1-2

Until this time Aviv had been the seventh month, but now G-d caused a rotation of the months. Aviv would be the first month instead of Tishri, and Tishri would be the seventh month instead of Aviv. This means that Tishri is the "Sabbatical" month, and it will relate very much to the weekly Sabbath. Here are the months as they are on the religious calendar:

The Religious Calendar

1. Nisan (Aviv)   7. Tishri (Ethanim)

2. Iyar (Zif)   8. Chesvan (Bul)

3. Sivan   9. Kislev

4. Tammuz   10. Tevet

5. Av   11. Sh'vat

6. Elul   12. Adar

As mentioned before, the festivals are figured from the religious calendar. The first three--Pesach, Hag HaMatzah, and Firstfruits are in Aviv. Shavuot is in Sivan. Finally, Yom Teruah, Yom Kippur, and Sukkot are found in Tishri. Just as the division of the festivals into two groups speaks of the work of Messiah in two comings, so do the two calendars. One calendar starts in spring, coinciding with the first coming, while the other one starts in the fall exactly six months later, coinciding with the second coming.

The Festivals on the Calendar

(Religious Calendar)

1. Pesach/Passover -	Aviv 14
2. Hag Ha Matzah/Unleavened Bread -	Aviv 15-21
3. Firstfruits of the Barley Harvest -	The Day after the Sabbath during Hag Ha Matzah
4. Shavuot/Weeks -	50 days after Firstfruits of the Barley
5. Yom Teruah (Rosh haShanah)/Trumpets -	Tishri 1
6. Yom Kippur/Atonement -	Tishri 10
7. Sukkot/Tabernacles -	Tishri 15-21

The Seven Thousand Year Plan of G-d

THE SEVEN THOUSAND YEAR PLAN
OF G-D

Another important element in understanding the festivals is being able to comprehend the seven thousand-year plan of G-d. In Genesis chapter One, G-d created the universe, and everything that dwells in it, in six, twenty-four hour days. Obviously, it would have been easily within the power of G-d to have finished all creation in a moment of time.[1] On the seventh day G-d rested and instituted the Sabbath (meaning rest). Without doubt, G-d was not tired; rather, He was already revealing to us His blueprint for the ages. In Colossians 2.16-17, which was discussed earlier, G-d told us that the weekly Sabbath is a picture of something to come, and that it would be centered in the Messiah. This is further developed in Hebrews four, where the Sabbath is interpreted three ways: as the literal weekly rest, as the rest that can be had by faith in Yeshua, and as the seventh day yet to come, a prophetic day.

> Let us therefore fear, lest, a promise being left us of entering into his rest, any of you should seem to come short of it. For unto us was the gospel preached, as well as unto them: but the word preached did not profit them, not being mixed with faith in them that heard it. For we which have believed do enter into rest, as he said, As I have sworn in my wrath, if they shall enter into my rest: although the works were finished from the foundation of the world. For he spake in a certain place of the seventh day on this wise, And G-d did rest the seventh day from all his works. And

---

1) Psa. 33.6-9

in this place again, if they shall enter into my rest. Seeing therefore it remaineth that some must enter therein, and they to whom it was first preached entered not in because of unbelief: Again, he limiteth a certain day, saying in David, Today, after so long a time; as it is said, Today if ye will hear his voice, harden not your hearts. For if Yeshua had given them rest, then would he not afterward have spoken of another day. There remaineth therefore a rest to the people of G-d.
Hebrews 4.1-9

The writer of this passage had previously quoted Psalm 95.7-11.[2] In verse 11 G-d says that those who rebel against Him cannot enter His rest. The word used for rest is the Hebrew word m'nuchah. This is the same word that is used in Isaiah.

And in that day (the Day of the L-rd) there shall be a root of Jesse, which shall stand for an ensign of the people; to it shall the Gentiles seek: and his rest shall be glorious.
Isaiah 11.10

This speaks of the rest in the Messianic Kingdom. The ancient Jewish prophets and scholars often spoke of this day. They related the seventh day to the Messianic Kingdom. On the Sabbath, Psalm ninety two is recited, today as it was by the Levites in the Temple at the offering of the tamid, the morning sacrifice. Rashi, a renowned Rabbi and commentator, explains the appropriateness of this Psalm for the Sabbath on the grounds that its portrayal of the world's perfection refers to how life will be in Messianic times. In Rabbinic tradition the "life of the world to come" is described as "a day that is completely Sabbath."[3] This seventh day in the Scriptures is often called "the Day of the L-rd."

2) Heb. 3.7-19

3) Hertz, Joseph, Daily Prayer Book (New York: Bloch Publishing Company.,1975) pg. 415

It was taught that this day, as well as each of the previous six days, would last for one thousand years.[4]

> For a thousand years in thy sight are but as yesterday when it is past, and as a watch in the night.
> Psalm 90.4

> But the heavens and the earth, which are now, by the same word are kept in store, reserved unto fire against the day of judgement and perdition of ungodly men. But, beloved, be not ignorant of this one thing, that one day is with the L-rd as a thousand years, and a thousand years as one day. The L-rd is not slack concerning his promise, as some men count slackness; but is longsuffering to us-ward, not willing that any should perish, but that all should come to repentance. But the Day of the L-rd will come as a thief in the night; in the which the heavens will pass away with a great noise, and the elements will melt with fervent heat, the earth also and the works that are therein shall be burned up.
> II Shimon (Peter) 3.7-10

> And I saw thrones, and they sat upon them, and judgment was given unto them: and I saw the souls of them that were beheaded for the witness of Yeshua, and for the word of G-d, and which had not worshipped the beast, neither his image, neither had received his mark upon their foreheads, or in their hands; and they lived and reigned with Messiah for a thousand years. But the rest of the dead lived not again until the thousand years were finished. This is the first resurrection. Blessed and holy is he that hath part in the first resurrection: on such the second death has no power, but they shall be priests of G-d and of Messiah, and shall reign with Him a thousand years.
> Revelation 20.4-6

The article entitled "Millennium" from *The Encyclopedia of the Jewish Religion*, edited by R.J. Zwi Werblowsky and Geoffrey Wigoder, 1986 by Adama Books, page 263; states that the belief

---

4)   Sanhedrin 97a; Avodah Zarah 9a

in each day of the week of creation represented a one thousand year day of G-d, with the seventh day being "the Day of the L-rd", or "millennium." This belief could first be found in the Slavic version of the pseudepigraphal Book of Enoch (33.1-2). It was further developed by the "tannaim" (the Rabbis shortly before, during, and immediately following Yeshua's lifetime), who based their interpretation on Psalm 90.4. They explained that as the days of creation were six in number, the world would last for six thousand years. The seventh "world day," the sabbath, was to be the one thousand years of the Messiah (Sanhedrin 97a; Avodah Zarah 9a).

The depictions of the seven thousand-year plan of G-d in the Scriptures are many. For example, Solomon, the Prince of Peace, in his wisdom, wealth, and glory was a shadow of the Messiah to come. Six steps (six thousand years) led to his throne (the thousand year kingdom).[5]

In the first two chapters of Yochanan, we have another picture of the seven thousand year plan of G-d. The key is to count the days before Yeshua went to the wedding in Cana. It is on the seventh day that Yeshua attended the wedding, a parallel to the wedding in the Messianic Kingdom. The first four days are found in verses 19, 29, 35 and 43 of Chapter One. On the fourth day, Yeshua takes a trip, and is not seen again until the seventh day in Chapter two.[6]

An interesting thing about this occurrence is that the journey Yeshua takes on the fourth day relates to Biblical chronology. Starting from creation, and counting the years from Adam to Noah's flood, from the flood to Abraham, from Abraham to

---

5) II Chr. 9.17-19

6) Jn. 1.19-2.3

Jacob's sojourn to Egypt, and so forth, it is apparent that the Messiah came into the world at the end of four thousand years (the fourth day), and He will return at the end of the six thousandth year (the beginning of the seventh day). There are many pictures similar to these, showing various things about the seven thousand-year plan of G-d. For example:

(1) Noah (Genesis 7.6)

(2) The Transfiguration (Mattatiyahu 17.1-9)

(3) The Coronation of Joash (II Kings 11)

(4) The seven years of Absalom (II Samuel 13-18)

(5) Isaac (Genesis 22-24)

Noah

Noah was 600 years old at the time of the flood. When the earth reaches 6,000 years, G-d will bring a judgment on the earth. This is the beginning of the Messianic Kingdom. Remember that one of the names of Rosh haShanah is Yom Ha Din, the Day of Judgment.

The Transfiguration

In Mattatiyahu (Matthew) 17.1-9, Yeshua is seen coming in glory with Moses and Elijah after six days (6,000 years). Several important messages about the Messianic Kingdom can be found in this passage. In the preceding passage, Mattatiyahu 16.27-28,

Yeshua promises His disciples that some of them will not see death till they see Him coming in His glory. Literally, this was fulfilled in the vision of the transfiguration.[7] The fact that the transfiguration takes place after six days is the picture of the six thousand years. In Yeshua's transfiguration into His glorified body, G-d promises those who believe in Yeshua a similar body.

> Beloved, now are we the sons of G-d, and it doth not yet appear what we shall be: but we know that, when He shall appear, we shall be like Him; for we shall see Him as He is.
> I Yochanan (John) 3.2

Another point to note is that Yeshua takes the three and brings them up into a high mountain apart.[8] At the end of the six thousand years the Messiah will gather those who are His disciples together in the Natzal (rapture).

> For the L-rd himself shall descend from heaven with a shout, with the voice of the archangel, and with the trump of G-d: and the dead in Messiah shall rise first: then we which are alive and remain shall be caught up together with them in the clouds, to meet the L-rd in the air: and so shall we ever be with the L-rd.
> I Thessalonians 4.16-17

Also, it is no mere coincidence that the two appearing with Yeshua in this vision from G-d are Elijah and Moses.[9] The messages communicated here are numerous. These two play a prominent role in Jewish eschatology concerning the coming wedding of the Messiah as the literal Kingdom begins. Each Jewish wedding requires two witnesses. These two are often the

---

7) Mt. 17.9

8) Mt. 17.1

9) Mt. 17.3

same as "the friends of the bridegroom," one assigned to the bride while the other is assigned to the groom. Yochanan the Immerser (John the Baptist), who is of the spirit of Elijah,[10] claimed to be one of these.

> Ye yourselves bear me witness, that I said, I am not the Messiah, but that I am sent before Him. He that hath the bride is the bridegroom: but the friend of the bridegroom, which standeth and heareth him, rejoiceth greatly because of the bridegroom's voice: this my joy therefore is fulfilled.
> Yochanan (John) 3.28-29

According to Jewish tradition, the other "friend of the bridegroom," is Moses. He is understood to be the one assigned to the bride. A function of this "friend of the bridegroom" is to escort the bride to her groom. The rabbis saw Moses in this role as he escorted Israel to Mount Sinai to meet with G-d for the betrothal.[11]

> And Moses brought forth the people out of the camp to meet with G-d; and they stood at the nether part of the mount.
> Exodus 19.17

Several places, these two are seen in the role as the witnesses. Following the resurrection of Yeshua, an incident occurs on the road to Emmaus where two followers of Yeshua are upset over His death. Not realizing that it is the risen Messiah that accompanies them, they share their heartache with Yeshua. Notice in His reply the reference to the two witnesses.

> Then He said unto them, O fools, and slow of heart to believe all that the prophets have spoken: ought not Messiah to have suffered these things, and to enter into His glory? And beginning

10) Lk. 1.17

11) Jer. 2.1-3

at Moses and all the prophets (personified in Elijah), he expounded unto them in all the Scriptures the things concerning Himself.

Luke 24.25-27

Indeed the Torah (Moses) and the Prophets (Elijah) are the two witnesses that testify that Yeshua is the salvation of G-d. The rabbis taught that before the Messiah would come G-d would send Elijah to prepare His way. This was based on four passages of scripture from the prophets.

Behold, I will send you Elijah the prophet before the coming of the great and dreadful day of the L-rd: and he shall turn the heart of the fathers to the children, and the heart of the children to their fathers, lest I come and smite the earth with a curse.

Malachi 4.5-6

Behold, I will send my messenger, and he shall prepare the way before me: and the L-rd, whom ye seek, shall suddenly come to his temple, even the messenger of the covenant, whom ye delight in: behold, he shall come, saith the L-rd of hosts.

Malachi 3.1

The voice of him that crieth in the wilderness, Prepare ye the way of the L-rd, make straight in the desert a highway for our G-d. Every valley shall be exalted, and every mountain and hill shall be made low: and the crooked shall be made straight, and the rough places plain: And the glory of the L-rd shall be revealed, and all flesh shall see it together: for the mouth of the L-rd hath spoken it.

Isaiah 40.3-5

Go through, go through the gates; prepare ye the way of the people; cast up, cast up the highway; gather out the stones; lift up a standard for the people. Behold, the L-rd hath proclaimed unto the end of the world, Say ye to the daughter of Zion, Behold, thy salvation cometh; behold, his reward is with him, and his work before him.

Isaiah 62.10-11

Coming down from the mountain, the disciples, having seen the vision and heard from G-d that Yeshua is the Messiah, ask about the coming of Elijah.[12] Yeshua's answer tells us of two Elijahs, one past and the other future.

> And Yeshua answered and said unto them, Elijah truly shall come first, and restore all things. But I say unto you, That Elijah is come already, and they knew him not, but have done unto him whatsoever they listed. Likewise shall also the Son of man suffer of them. Then the disciples understood that He spake unto them of Yochanan the Immerser.
>
> Mattatiyahu (Matthew) 17.11-13

This future coming of Elijah [in reality one who has the commission of Elijah just as Yochanan (John) had, but not really the man] is spoken of in the book of Revelation.

> And I will give power unto my two witnesses, and they shall prophesy a thousand two hundred and threescore days (three and a half years), clothed in sackcloth. These are the two olive trees, and the two candlesticks standing before the G-d of the earth. And if any man will hurt them, fire proceedeth out of their mouth, and devoureth their enemies: and if any man will hurt them, he must in this manner be killed. These have power to shut heaven, that it rain not in the days of their prophecy: and have power over waters to turn them to blood, and to smite the earth with all plagues, as often as they will. And when they shall have finished their testimony, the beast that ascendeth out of the bottomless pit shall make war against them and shall overcome them, and kill them.
>
> Revelation 11.3-7

That this passage is speaking of the future Moses and Elijah can easily be seen by the parallel between the actions of these two witnesses and the original Moses and Elijah. The ancient Elijah had shut up the heavens for three and a half years and called down

---

12) Mt. 17.10

fire from heaven to kill the one hundred and two soldiers of King Ahaziah. Moses, in his day, had turned the waters to blood and called down ten separate plagues upon Egypt.

Remember that the purpose for these two witnesses is that they personify the scriptures that testify to the working of G-d through Yeshua the Messiah.

The Coronation of Joash

The coronation of the rightful King at the end of six years corresponds to Yeshua's coronation at the end of six thousand years. Also seen in this passage is the glory of the Kingdom and the judgment of the false ruler.

II Kings eleven has become one of the most important passages in the Bible to the student of the Messianic Kingdom. It is only here and in the coronation of Solomon that the scriptures provide us with a look into the Jewish coronation ceremony. It is strange how little attention is paid to the aspect of the Messiah as King, especially from the necessary Jewish vantage point. The Messiah will be crowned at the beginning of the thousand year kingdom, as told to us by the prophet Daniel.

> I saw in the night visions, and, behold, one like the Son of man came with the clouds of heaven, and came to the Ancient of days, and they brought Him near before Him. And there was given Him dominion, and glory, and a kingdom, that all people, nations, and languages should serve Him: His dominion is an everlasting dominion, which shall not pass away, and His kingdom that which shall not be destroyed.
> Daniel 7.13-14

Joash is a type of the Messiah and is thus presented as being hid in the House of the L-rd for six years (six thousand).

And He was with her hid in the House of the L-rd six years. And
Athaliah did reign over the land.
II Kings 11.3

Even as Joash is a picture of Yeshua, Athaliah who rules for
the same six years is a picture of Satan and his rule. However, in
the seventh year, Jehoiada, the High Priest, calls for the nobles
of the land and commanders of the army. Within the Temple of
the L-rd, He reveals to them the rightful heir to the throne.

And the seventh year Jehoiada sent and fetched the rulers over
hundreds, with the captains and the guard, and brought them to
him into the House of the L-rd, and made a covenant with them,
and took an oath of them in the House of the L-rd, and showed
them the King's son.
II Kings 11.4

Three points should be seen in the above passage: the time
of the coronation, that the coronation will take place in the
Temple (Heavenly) of the L-rd, and the revealing of the Messiah.

And the guard stood, every man with his weapons in his hand,
round about the King, from the right corner of the Temple to the
left corner of the Temple, along by the altar and the Temple. And
he brought forth the King's son, and put the crown upon Him,
and gave Him the testimony; and they made Him King, and
anointed Him; and they clapped their hands, and said, G-d save
the King.
II Kings 11.11-12

Note that not only is the King given the "crown" but also the
"testimony." This "testimony" or "solemn law" is probably also part
of the insignia of the king, representing his authority. In
comparing other passages of Scripture, the "testimony" might be
the same as the "bracelets" of King Saul, delivered to David along

with his "crown" following Saul's death.[13] Or possibly it is the "decree" that is issued in Psalm two (a "coronation Psalm"), as the Son is crowned. In the passage above from Daniel 7.13-14, the "dominion" that is delivered to the Messiah is probably referring to some insignia denoting His authority.

The coronation ceremony included four other parts in addition to the investiture with the insignia. These were the anointing, acclamation, enthronement, and the homage. The king was presented before the people, and had oil poured over his head by the High Priest. The oil symbolized that the Ruach haKodesh (the Holy Spirit) had taken hold of the king, empowering him as the servant of G-d on behalf of His people. For this reason the king is referred to as the "anointed of the L-rd".[14] The Hebrew word "Mashiach" (Messiah) means anointed; therefore, each king, in a sense, was seen as a messiah. Through this, G-d was preparing us for the "Anointed One" yet to come.

In the passage concerning Joash, all the people cry out, "G-d save the King." In this, it is not intended that the people have chosen the king, but rather that they have accepted the choice made by the L-rd, now made effective by the anointing.

The next part of the coronation ceremony, the enthronement, is witnessed in the following passage.

> And he took the rulers over hundreds, and the captains, and the guard, and all the people of the land; and they brought down the king from the House of the L-rd, and came by the way of the gate

---

13) II Samuel 1.10

14) I Sam. 24.6,10; 26.9,11,16, 23; II Sam. 1.14,16; 19.21

of the guard to the king's house. And he sat on the throne of the kings.

II Kings 11.19

This action marks his assumption of power. "To sit on the throne" is synonymous for "to begin to reign." As the L-rd was held to be the true king of Israel, the royal throne is called the throne of the L-rd[15] and had Justice and Right for its supports.[16] Following the king's possession of the throne, the high officials of the kingdom come to do homage to him,[17] thereby pledging their loyalty and he confirming their offices. It is with this understanding that the Messianic throne is looked forward to. The prophet Zechariah foretold of the throne of King Messiah, who would not only be a king but also the High Priest.

And speak unto him, saying, Thus speaketh the L-rd of hosts, saying, Behold the man whose name is The Branch; and He shall grow up out of His place, and He shall build the Temple of the L-rd: Even He shall build the Temple of the L-rd; and He shall bear the glory, and shall sit and rule upon His throne; and He shall be a priest upon His throne: and the counsel of peace shall be between them both.

Zechariah 6.12-13

And it shall come to pass in the last day, that the mountain of the L-rd's House shall be established in the top of the mountains, and shall be exalted above the hills; and all nations shall flow unto it. And many people shall go and say, Come ye, and let us go up to the mountain of the L-rd, to the House of the G-d of Jacob; and he will teach us of His ways, and we will walk in His paths: for out of Zion shall go forth the Torah (law), and the word of the L-rd from Jerusalem. And He shall judge among the nations, and shall rebuke many people: and they shall beat their

---

15) I Chr. 29.23

16) Psa. 89.15; 97.2

17) I Kgs. 1.47

swords into plowshares, and their spears into pruning hooks:
nation shall not lift up sword against nation, neither shall they
learn war any more.

Isaiah 2.2-4

Absalom

The story of Absalom (II Samuel 13-18) is full of insights into
the Messianic Kingdom. Absalom is one of the best pictures of
the rebellion of the false messiah in the scriptures. The story
begins in II Samuel thirteen with the sin of Amnon. Amnon is the
firstborn son of David, making him the crown prince. A parallel
can be drawn here to Adam, the first man and crown prince of
G-d. Amnon desires that which is forbidden, Tamar, his
half-sister, even as Adam desired to eat of the tree of knowledge.
A tempter, Jonadab, encourages Amnon in the transgression
even as the serpent did likewise in the Garden of Eden. Amnon
sins, following the pattern of Adam, thereby setting in motion the
next seven years which ends in the death of Absalom, following
his rebellion. Absalom, the brother of Tamar and half-brother of
Amnon, begins to show his deceitful heart from the beginning.

And Absalom spake unto his brother Amnon neither good nor
bad: for Absalom hated Amnon, because he had forced his sister
Tamar.

II Samuel 13.22

Absalom waits two years to strike Amnon.[18]

Ye are of your father the devil, and the lusts of your father ye will
do: he was a murderer from the beginning, and abode not in the
truth, because there is no truth in him. When he speaketh a lie,
he speaketh of his own: for he is a liar, and the father of it.

Yochanan (John) 8.44

18) II Sam. 13.23-29

Following the slaying of Amnon, Absalom flees to another kingdom and remains there for three years, now a total of five years.[19] In contrast to the heart of Absalom is that of David, who wants to see his son restored, even though he has murdered his firstborn. Through the actions of Joab, Absalom is allowed to return to Jerusalem, but for two years will not be able to see the king himself.[20] At this point, seven years into the story, Absalom is restored to the king.

Chapter fifteen of II Samuel begins with Absalom's undermining the support of David among the people of Israel. It seems that most of the people are deceived by his royal appearance, and by his ability to tell each person what he was wanting to hear. A plot is hatched by Absalom to take the kingdom from his father. A direct parallel is seen between the actions of Absalom and the false Messiah of the future, who at the beginning of the seventh day also tries to take the kingdom from the true king. Absalom has a co-conspirator in Ahithophel, just as the false messiah has his false prophet.[21]

Several traits of Absalom are helpful in seeing the picture of the false messiah. The name "Absalom" means "Father of Peace," while his nature shows him to be the most cold-hearted of men. Yeshua, in the Olivet discourse, warned of the one to come:

> For many shall come in my name, saying, I am Messiah; and shall deceive many.
>
> Mattatiyahu (Matthew) 24.5

The very appearance of Absalom is also a glimpse of the false Messiah.

---

19) II Sam. 13.38

20) II Sam. 14.23-33

21) Rev. thirteen

> But in all Israel there was none to be so much praised as Absalom for his beauty: from the sole of his foot even to the crown of his head there was no blemish in him. And when he polled his head, (for it was at every year's end that he polled it: because the hair was heavy on him, therefore he polled it:) he weighed the hair of his head at two hundred shekels after the king's weight.
>
> II Samuel 14.25-26

Note that not only does the passage describe his beauty, but also goes into detail about his covering (hair). Remember that the strength of Sampson was his hair. The understanding with Sampson was that the hair represented G-d for he was forbidden by G-d (because He was a Nazarite) to cut it. With Absalom, however, it is a matter of pride. His covering was his own vanity. The prophet Ezekiel, in describing Satan, also alluded to his beauty.

> Thine heart was lifted up because of thy beauty, thou hast corrupted thy wisdom by reason of thy brightness: I will cast thee to the ground, I will lay thee before kings, that they may behold thee.
>
> Ezekiel 28.17

How opposite is this man to the true Messiah who is presented in Isaiah fifty three.

> For He shall grow up before Him as a tender plant, and as a root out of a dry ground: he hath no form nor comeliness; and when we shall see him, there is no beauty that we should desire Him.
>
> Isaiah 53.2

As Absalom approaches the city of Jerusalem, David flees into the wilderness. In the last days, the Jewish believers in Yeshua will also flee into the wilderness with the false messiah's approach. Absalom has it in his heart to kill his father and all that are with him. By parallel, the false messiah will make war against the saints.[22]

In the ensuing war, Absalom is defeated and dies a unique death, for he is caught by his hair (his covering) in the branch of a tree. In numerous passages of scripture, the "Branch" is a term for the Messiah.[23] Therefore, his own pride became his downfall, just as the false messiah deceives himself into believing that he can defeat the G-d of heaven or His Messiah.

Isaac

Isaac, possibly more than any other personality within the Bible, portrays the Messiah. From his birth he is seen as the promised son.

> And, behold, the word of the L-rd came unto him, saying, This shall not be thine heir; but he that shall come forth out of thine own bowels shall be thine heir.
> Genesis 15.4

> And He said; I will certainly return unto thee according to the time of life, and lo, Sarah thy wife shall have a son. And Sarah heard it in the tent door, which was behind Him.
> Genesis 18.10

> And the L-rd visited Sarah as He had said, and the L-rd did unto Sarah as He had spoken. For Sarah conceived, and bare Abraham a son in his old age, at the set time of which G-d had spoken to him.
> Genesis 21.1-2

The Torah readings for both days of Rosh haShanah are about Isaac. The main reading is known as the "akeida," which

---

22) Rev. 13.7

23) Isa. 11.1-2, Jer. 23.5-6; 33.15-16; Zech. 3.8-9; 6.10-13

means "the binding of the sacrifice," and is taken from Genesis twenty two. The passage begins with G-d telling Abraham to go to the land of Moriah. There he is to offer his beloved son Isaac as an "olah," or "burnt offering." The land of Moriah is interesting, as this is where G-d will have Solomon build the Temple. It was also the place purchased by King David to offer sacrifice after he had sinned in numbering the people.[24] The fact that Abraham is called upon to offer Isaac as an "olah" rather than one of the other sacrifices is important, for an "olah" is offered with a willing heart. Genesis 22.4 says that on the third day Abraham saw the place afar off. It is true that he saw Moriah, but could he have seen more? Notice in the context of this chapter, it refers to "seeing." This will be commented upon shortly. Often people have an idea that Isaac was just a small boy, when in reality he was a full grown man submitting to his father's wish. Just as the wood was laid upon Yeshua, so will the wood be laid upon Isaac. To Isaac's question of where is the lamb, Abraham replies that G-d will provide Himself, a lamb for a burnt offering. As he raises the knife to slay Isaac, he is stopped by the angel of the L-rd. G-d has provided a ram caught in a thicket (in Judaism the thicket is said to be the sins of the people) for Abraham to substitute for Isaac.

The parallels with Yeshua are many. He is the beloved son of the father. Yeshua willingly laid down His own life. He was sacrificed on Mount Moriah. He died for the sins of the people, and He that went forth to die came again in life.

Abraham called the place "Adonai Yireh,"[25] which means "In the Mount of the L-rd it will be seen." Not only did he see Yeshua's death, burial, and resurrection, but He also saw all the

---

24) II Chr. 3.1

25) Gen. 22.14

way to the end of the Messianic Kingdom to the period of time called the Olam Haba (the World to Come).

> By faith Abraham, when he was called to go out into a place which he should after receive for an inheritance, obeyed; and he went out, not knowing whither he went. By faith he sojourned in the land of promise, as in a strange country, dwelling in tabernacles with Isaac and Jacob, the heirs with him of the same promise: For he looked for a city which hath foundations, whose builder and maker is G-d. Through faith also Sarah herself received strength to conceive seed, and was delivered of a child when she was past age, because she judged him faithful who had promised. Therefore sprang there even of one, and him as good as dead, so many as the stars of the sky in multitude, and as the sand which is by the sea shore innumerable. These all died in faith, not having received the promises, but having seen them afar off, and were persuaded of them, and embraced them, and confessed that they were strangers and pilgrims on the earth. For they that say such things declare plainly that they seek a country. And truly, if they had been mindful of that country from whence they came out, they might have had opportunity to have returned. But now they desire a better country, that is, an heavenly: wherefore G-d is not ashamed to be called their G-d: for he hath prepared for them a city.
>
> Hebrews 11.8-16

Yeshua referred to this when he said:

> Your father Abraham rejoiced to see my day: and he saw it, and was glad.
>
> Yochanan (John) 8.56

Again, pictures of the Messiah are found with Isaac in Genesis Twenty-four, in which Eliezer, the servant of Abraham, is sent to secure a bride for him. As the wedding customs are covered in chapter eleven of the text, the reader is referred there. The key is that this chapter should be read seeing Isaac as Yeshua, Rebekah (the bride) as the believers, and Eliezer as the Ruach haKodesh (the Holy Spirit).

The Seven Thousand Year Plan of G-d   **77**

Isaac, being married at forty,[26] relates to Yeshua's coming to earth at the end of four thousand years to take out a bride for Himself; whereas, the birth of His children at sixty[27] shows the salvation of His people at the end of six thousand years.

Yeshua paid the price for His bride when the world was approximately 4,000 years old. Isaac had children when he was sixty. At the end of the 6,000 years, the nation of Israel will be brought to birth in the Messiah. This is why many passages dealing with the beginning of the Messianic Kingdom also speak of the birthpangs of a woman.

Walter K. Price, in his book *Next Year in Jerusalem*, entitled a chapter "Birthpains of the Messiah." His book is unusual for one who believes in Yeshua, for he broke away from many of the Christian stereotypes in talking about Bible prophecy. In his examination of Jewish eschatology, he found a great deal of material on a period of time preceding the Messiah's coming known as the "birthpangs." Rabbinic literature abounded with references to this period. The term "Birthpains of the Messiah" does not mean that the Messiah is being born into the world, but rather that the world will go through a time of trouble so intense shortly before His coming that it is compared to a woman in labor. Most Christians call this time the tribulation, but in all probability it was called the "birthpangs" by Yeshua as well as his followers.

As mentioned, there are many other types and shadows that continue to show that at the end of six thousand years (six days), G-d will begin his one thousand year Messianic Kingdom (the seventh day, the Sabbath of G-d).

The Messianic Kingdom should begin at the festival of Rosh

---

26) Gen. 25.20

27) Gen. 25.26

haShanah. Recall that creation began on Tishri 1 (Yom Teruah, Rosh haShanah). If G-d desires to finish six thousand years to the day, and then begin His Messianic Kingdom, it would fall on Tishri 1, the day He gave to teach about the beginning of the Messianic Kingdom. In fact, the Kingdom's beginning on a Rosh haShanah is a good probability rather than speculation. As the information unfolds, this should become more evident. Support for this idea is found in this portion from the Talmud.

> It has been taught: Rabbi Eliezer says, 'in the month of Tishri the world was created,...and in Tishri they will be redeemed in time to come.'
> Rosh haShanah 10b-11a

Chapter 6

Yom Teruah - Rosh haShanah

CHAPTER 6

YOM TERUAH--ROSH HASHANAH

In the Bible this festival is known as the Festival of the Blowing of Trumpets:

> And the L-rd spake unto Moses, saying, Speak unto the children of Israel, saying, In the seventh month (Tishri on the religious calendar), on the first day of the month, shall ye have a Sabbath, a memorial of blowing of trumpets, a holy convocation. Ye shall do no servile work therein: but ye shall offer an offering made by fire unto the L-rd.
>
> Leviticus 23.23-25

> It is a day of blowing the trumpets unto you.
> Numbers 29.1

According to the Mishnah[1] the trumpet used for this purpose is the shofar or ram's horn, not trumpets made of metal as in Numbers ten. The shofar was used to announce the beginning of festivals,[2] to muster troops,[3] to warn of danger,[4] to assemble the people, in the midst of battles,[5] and for coronations.[6]

The Gesenius Hebrew Lexicon states that the word, "teruah," is an awakening blast. This theme of awakening is often associated

---

1) Rosh haShanah 16a; Rosh haShanah 3.3; Num. 29.1

2) Psa. 81.3

3) Rosh haShanah 3.4

4) ibid

5) Rosh haShanah 3.4

6) I Kings 1.34,39

with Rosh haShanah. Many times this refers to mankind's hearing the blast of the shofar and repenting of their sins before Rosh haShanah, the Day of Judgment, arrives.

> Awake you sleepers from your sleep, and you slumberers, arise from your slumber -- examine your deeds, repent and remember your Creator. Those of you who forget the truth in the vanities of the times and dwell all year in vanity and emptiness, look into your souls, improve your ways and actions, let each of you forsake his evil path and his thoughts which are not good.
> Rambam, Hilchot Teshuvah, Chapter 3

Rav Shaul (Apostle Paul) in his letter to the Ephesians expressed this same message. More than likely, this and the following quote were drawn from an ancient Temple prayer for Rosh haShanah.

> Wherefore he saith, awake thou that sleepest, and arise from the dead, and Messiah shall give thee light. See then that ye walk circumspectly, not as fools, but as wise, redeeming the time, because the days are evil. Wherefore be ye not unwise, but understanding what the will of the L-rd is.
> Ephesian 5.14-17

In addition to calling to repent with the blast of the shofar, the awakening was also associated with the coming of the Messiah.

> Awake, awake, put on strength, O arm of the L-rd; awake, as in the ancient days, in the generations of old. Art thou not it that hath cut Rahab, and wounded the dragon?
> Isaiah 51.9

According to Rav Se'adiah Gaon, there are ten symbolic meanings for the sounding of the shofar.

"1. The day marks Creation's beginning; thereon G-d created the world and became its Sovereign. And at the beginning of a reign, it is customary to sound trumpets before the newly crowned king, and to proclaim his ascent to sovereignty throughout the realm. Similarly do we accept the Creator's sovereignty upon ourselves.

"2. Rosh Hashanah is the first of the Ten Days of Repentance, 'asseret yemei teshuvah', and shofar is sounded thereon to proclaim and to warn: Whoever wishes to repent -- let him repent; if not, let him have remorse later. And this is the way of kings; first they forewarn the people through decrees, and whoever transgresses has no complaint.

"3. To remind us of the stand at Mt. Sinai, of which it was said, 'And the sound of the shofar was exceedingly strong.' So that we might accept upon ourselves what our fathers accepted when they said, 'We will do and we will hear (understand and accept).'(Exodus 19.8,16-25)

"4. To remind us of the words of the 'Nevi'im' (the prophets), which were compared to the sounding of a shofar: -- 'And whoever hears the sound of the shofar (i.e. the call of the Prophets) and takes no warning -- if the sword comes and takes him away, his blood shall be upon his own head; whereas, if he had taken warning, he would have saved his soul' (Ezekiel 33.1-7).

"5. To remind us of the destruction of 'Beit Hamikdash' (the Sanctuary in Jerusalem) and the trumpet-blasting of the enemy attack. When we hear the shofar's sound, we are to pray to G-d for the rebuilding of the Sanctuary.

"6. To remind us, through the sounding of a ram's horn, of the binding of Itzchak (the 'Akedah'), who offered his life to G-d, and of the ram slaughtered in his place. Likewise, are we to offer our lives for the sanctification of His Name, so that our remembrance may ascend before Him for the good.

"7. When we hear the sound of the shofar, we are to feel fear and trembling, and are to humble ourselves before the Creator. For this is the effect of the shofar -- that it arouses fright and trembling, as it is written: 'If a shofar is sounded in the city, shall the people not tremble?' (Amos three).

"8. To recall in fear the forthcoming great Day of Judgment, as it is said: 'Near is the great day of the L-rd, near and exceedingly soon is the day of shofar and shouting' (Zephaniah one).

"9. To recall our faith in the future ingathering of Israel's dispersed, and to awaken our yearning for it. As it is said: 'And it shall be on that day -- a great shofar will be sounded, and those who have perished in the land of Assyria, and those who were dispersed in the land of Egypt will come...' (Isaiah twenty-seven).

"10. To recall our faith in the future resurrection of the dead. As it is said: 'All you inhabitants of the world, and you who dwell in the earth; when an ensign is lifted on the mountains you shall see, and when the shofar is sounded you shall hear' (Isaiah eighteen)."

As it has been demonstrated, the day is the first day on the civil calendar. Therefore, it is celebrated as the Jewish New Year. It is a time of initiation and renewal. It is the time of reconciling oneself to G-d and to one's fellow men. It is a time for rededication and recommitment to G-d and His ways.

Another name for the festival is Yom HaZikkaron, "Day of

Remembrance." Yom haZikkaron, the Day of Remembrance, is both a Biblical and Talmudic term for Rosh haShanah. In the Bible it is found in Leviticus twenty-three.

Speak unto the children of Israel, saying, In the seventh month, in the first day of the month, shall ye have a sabbath, a memorial (zikkaron) of blowing of trumpets, a holy convocation.
Leviticus 23.24

In the Talmud, as well as the liturgy for Rosh haShanah, the term plays a prominent part. The creation of G-d, as well as His relationship with His people, is brought into focus. During the Rosh haShanah service, a portion is known as "Zikhronot -- that portion of the Mussaf of the New Year's Day which deals with Divine remembrance. Several books are opened by G-d on Rosh haShanah. One of these is known as the Book of Remembrance.

Then they that feared the L-rd spake often one to another: and the L-rd hearkened, and heard it, and a book of remembrance was written before him for them that feared the L-rd, and that thought upon his name.
Malachi 3.16

This Book of Remembrance surely ties in with an event that follows the Natzal (catching away of the believers). Along with the coronation and the marriage, there is also a rewarding of the believers. Rav Shaul (the apostle Paul) referred to this in the following passages:

But why dost thou judge thy brother? or why dost thou set at naught thy brother? for we shall all stand before the judgment seat of Messiah.
Romans 14.10

For we are labourers together with G-d: ye are G-d's husbandry, ye are G-d's building. According to the grace of G-d which is given unto me, as a wise masterbuilder, I have laid the foundation, and another buildeth thereon. But let every man take

heed how he buildeth thereupon. For other foundation can no man lay than that is laid, which is Yeshua haMashiach. Now if any man build upon this foundation gold, silver, precious stones, wood, hay, stubble; Every man's work shall be made manifest: for the day shall declare it, because it shall be revealed by fire; and the fire shall try every man's work of what sort it is. If any man's work abide which he hath built thereupon, he shall receive a reward. If any man's work shall be burned, he shall suffer loss: but he himself shall be saved; yet so as by fire.
I Corinthians 3.9-15

For we must all appear before the judgment seat of Messiah; that every one may receive the things done in his body, according to that he hath done, whether it be good or bad.
II Corinthians 5.10

It is a day for Israel to remember her G-d and all that He is and does. It is the day G-d remembers His people. It is on this day, as shall be demonstrated elsewhere, that G-d will open the Book of Life, and hold a trial.[7] Those who have accepted the Messiah will be remembered for good; those who have not, for evil.

The festival of Rosh haShanah encompasses many themes and teaches many doctrines. The topics that will be discussed in the following chapters are teshuvah--repentance, the time of Jacob's trouble, the resurrection of the dead, the natzal (plucking away), the coronation of the Messiah, the beginning of the Messianic Kingdom, the judgment, and the wedding of the Messiah.

---

7) Rosh haShanah 16b

CHAPTER 7

TESHUVAH

On the Jewish calendar there is a forty-day season called Teshuvah (meaning return, or repentance).

Repentance, in Hebrew, is known as "teshuvah," which literally means "to return."

This season, beginning on Elul 1 and concluding on Tishri 10 (Yom Kippur), lasts for forty days. Without an understanding of the message of this season, it is impossible to fully grasp the meaning of the High Holy Days (Rosh haShanah to Yom Kippur).

According to the rabbis, man is born with an evil inclination, or a tendency to sin, of which repentance is the anti-dote. Repentance means more than just turning from one's sins; it is a return to G-d and to the right path. In the Talmud, repentance is regarded as one of the seven things created by G-d before he created the world.[1] The desire of G-d is that all repent and not face the penalty for sin.

> The L-rd is not slack concerning His promise, as some men count slackness; but is longsuffering to us-ward, not willing that any should perish, but that all should come to repentance.
> II Shimon (Peter) 3.9

> But if the wicked will turn from all his sins that he hath committed, and keep all my statutes, and do that which is lawful and right, he shall surely live, he shall not die. All his transgressions that he hath committed, they shall not be mentioned unto him: in his

---

1) Pesachim 54a

righteousness that he hath done he shall live. Have I any pleasure at all that the wicked should die? saith the L-rd G-d: and not that he should return from his ways, and live?

Therefore I will judge you, O house of Israel, every one according to his ways, saith the L-rd G-d. Repent, and turn yourselves from all your transgressions; so iniquity shall not be your ruin. Cast away from you all your transgressions, whereby ye have transgressed; and make you a new heart and a new spirit: for why will ye die, O house of Israel? For I have no pleasure in the death of him that dieth, saith the L-rd G-d: wherefore turn yourselves, and live ye.

Ezekiel 18.21-23,30-32

In Judaism, a distinction is made between repentance for sins committed against G-d and those committed against one's fellow man. For this reason the Torah has two different sacrifices dealing with sin. The first was known as "hataat," the sin offering, while the other is called "asham," the guilt offering. The sin offering taught that when man sinned against G-d, restitution must be made with G-d; whereas, the guilt offering concerned man's restoring his relationship with another man before G-d. If a person sinned against another person, forgiveness would not be given by G-d if the guilty party only confessed his sin to G-d. He must first make restitution with his fellow man and then come to G-d. Yeshua referred to this in the book of Mattatiyahu (Matthew).

Therefore if thou bring thy gift to the altar, and there rememberest that thy brother hath aught against thee; leave there thy gift before the altar, and go thy way; first be reconciled to thy brother, and then come and offer thy gift.

Mattatiyahu (Matthew) 5.23-24

The season of Teshuvah is a time for each man to annually examine his own life. It is a time to restore relationships between men as well as G-d. Realizing that Rosh haShanah is understood as "The Day of Judgment" in which the heavenly court sits to review each man, repentance, therefore, becomes a pressing matter. The whole structure of the month of Elul is to turn one back toward G-d before that day arrives. As mentioned, this is carried out on an annual basis, but at the same time it is seen as being the plan of G-d before the advent of the eschatological Rosh haShanah that inaugurates the Day for the L-rd.

> Gather yourselves together, yea, gather together, O nation not desired; before the decree bring forth, before the day pass as the chaff, before the fierce anger of the L-rd come upon you, before the day of the L-rd's anger come upon you. Seek ye the L-rd, all ye meek of the earth, which have wrought his judgement; seek righteousness, seek meekness: it may be ye shall be hid in the day of the L-rd's anger.
> Zephaniah 2.1-3

In most Jewish communities, Psalm Twenty-seven, which the Midrash interprets as referring to "the Days of Awe" (from Rosh haShanah until Yom Kippur), is recited twice a day from Elul 1 until Shemini Atzeret (the festival that is on the 22nd of Tishri that follows Sukkot, and is known as the eighth day). Also, the shofar is blown each morning following the Shacharit (the morning prayers) to warn each individual to turn back to G-d. During the month, the book of Psalms is read through twice in most communities. It is customary, when writing a letter during Elul, to include wishes for the recipient's well-being in the next year and for his receiving a good judgment on Rosh haShanah. Special prayers called "selichot" (penitential prayers) begin to be said about one week before Rosh haShanah. Each individual searches his own heart and returns to the L-rd.

On the day of Rosh haShanah, each man is judged. G-d has three books that are opened. Those who have returned to G-d are written in the Book of the Righteous. Remember Yeshua's statement:

Yeshua saith unto him, I am the way, the truth, and the life: no
man cometh unto the Father, but by me.
Yochanan (John) 14.6

All other people are divided into two other groups. The first
of these is known as the Rashim, the wholly wicked, and their
names are written into a book of the same name. Their fate is
sealed on Rosh haShanah, for they have forever rejected, of their
own accord, the salvation of G-d provided through His Messiah.

The last group is known as the intermediates. These are the
common people, and they comprise the largest group. They have
not yet been judged righteous nor have they been placed into the
book of the wholly wicked. They are given ten more days to
repent. If they repent by Yom Kippur, they are written in the
Book of the Righteous; if not, they are listed with the wicked.
Their final fate is sealed on Yom Kippur.

The last chapter of Hosea conveys not only the theme of the
season of "Teshuvah," but also the prophetic promise to Israel
concerning it.

O Israel, return unto the L-rd thy G-d; for thou hast fallen by thine
iniquity. Take with you words, and turn to the L-rd: say unto Him,
Take away all iniquity, and receive us graciously: so will we
render the calves of our lips. Asshur shall not save us; we will
not ride upon horses: neither will we say any more to the work
of our hands, Ye are our G-ds: for in thee the fatherless find
mercy. I will heal their backsliding, I will love them freely: for mine
anger is turned away from him. I will be as the dew unto Israel:
he shall grow as the lily, and cast forth his roots as Lebanon. His
branches shall spread, and his beauty shall be as the olive tree,
and his smell as Lebanon. They that dwell under His shadow
shall return; they shall revive as the corn, and grow as the vine:
the scent thereof shall be as the wine of Lebanon. Ephraim shall
say, What have I to do any more with idols? I have heard Him,
and observed Him: I am like a green fir tree. From Me is thy fruit

found. Who is wise, and he shall understand these things? prudent and he shall know them? for the ways of the L-rd are right, and the just shall walk in them: but the transgressors shall fall therein.

Hosea 14.1-9

As mentioned, the season of Teshuvah starts on the first day of the twelfth month of the civil calendar -- Elul; includes Rosh haShanah; and goes until Yom Kippur, the tenth day of the first month. The last ten days (from Rosh haShanah to Yom Kippur) are known as the High Holy Days, the most sacred time of the Jewish year. Another name for this ten-day period is Yamim Nora'im (the Days of Awe), for at this time each person becomes accountable to G-d for his sins. Rosh haShanah is also known as Yom HaDin (the Day of Judgment). On this day, it is taught, all the inhabitants of the world pass before G-d. Each man is weighed in the balance and placed into one of three categories.[2]

> All things are judged on Rosh haShanah, and their fate is sealed on Yom Kippur, are the words of Rabbi Meir. Rabbi Judah, in the name of Rabbi Akiva, says: All things are judged on Rosh haShanah...
>
> Tosefta Rosh haShanah I.13

> It has been taught: The school of Shammai says: There will be three classes on the final Day of Judgement, one of the wholly righteous, one of the wholly wicked, and one of the intermediates. The wholly righteous are at once inscribed and sealed for life in the world to come; the wholly wicked are at once inscribed and sealed for Gehinnon perdition)...
>
> Rosh haShanah 16b-17a

> For this reason it is fit that we celebrate the Rosh haShanah as a festive day; but since it is a Day of Judgement for all living

---

2) Rosh haShanah 6b

things, it is also fit that we observe Rosh haShanah with greater
fear and awe than all the other festive days.
Sefer Ha-Hinukh, Mitzvah 311

Because Rosh haShanah is the Day of Judgment, awe and
even dread are a part of its message. Each day of the preceding
month, Elul, a shofar is blown following the morning service
(Shacharit). The shofar is blown to warn the people that Rosh
haShanah is approaching and that this is the season for
repentance.[3] Psalm Twenty-seven is read aloud, and in many
Jewish communities Ezekiel 33.1-7 is also read.

The L-rd is my light and my salvation; whom shall I fear? The L-
rd is the strength of my life; of whom shall I be afraid? When the
wicked, even mine enemies and my foes, came upon me to eat
up my flesh, they stumbled and fell. Though an host should
encamp against me, my heart shall not fear: though war should
rise against me, in this will I be confident. One thing have I
desired of the L-rd, that will I seek after; that I may dwell in the
house of the L-rd all the days of my life, to behold the beauty of
the L-rd, and to inquire in His temple. For in the time of trouble
he shall hide me in his pavillion: in the secret of his tabernacle
shall he hide me; he shall set me up upon a rock. And now shall
mine head be lifted up above mine enemies round about me:
therefore will I offer in his tabernacle sacrifices of joy; I will sing,
yea, I will sing praises unto the L-rd. Hear, O L-rd, when I cry with
my voice: have mercy also upon me, and answer me. When thou
saidst, Seek ye my face; my heart said unto thee, Thy face, L-rd,
will I seek. Hide not thy face far from me; put not thy servant
away in anger: thou hast been my help; leave me not neither
forsake me, O G-d of my salvation. When my father and my
mother forsake me, then the L-rd will take me up. Teach me thy
way, O L-rd, and lead me in a plain path, because of mine
enemies. Deliver me not over unto the will of mine enemies: for
false witnesses are risen up against me, and such as breathe out
cruelty. I had fainted, unless I had believed to see the goodness

3) Hilichot Teshuvah 3.4

of the L-rd in the land of the living. Wait on the L-rd: be of good
courage, and he shall strengthen thine heart: wait, I say, on the
L-rd.

Again the word of the L-rd came unto me, saying, Son of man,
speak to the children of thy people, and say unto them, When I
bring the sword upon a land, if the people of the land take a man
of their coasts, and set him for their watchman: if when he seeth
the sword come upon the land, he blow the trumpet, and warn
the people; Then whosoever heareth the sound of the trumpet,
and taketh not warning; if the sword come, and take him away,
his blood shall be upon his own head. He heard the sound of the
trumpet, and took not warning; his blood shall be upon him. But
he that taketh warning shall deliver his soul. But if the watchman
see the sword come, and blow not the trumpet, and the people
be not warned; if the sword come, and take any person from
among them, he is taken away in his iniquity; but his blood will I
require at the watchman's hand. So thou, O son of man, I have
set thee a watchman unto the house of Israel; therefore thou
shalt hear the word at my mouth, and warn them from me.
EZEKIEL 33.1-7

What stands out in Ezekiel so profoundly is that the
watchman on the wall is to warn the people of coming judgment
-- a sword upon the land. The call was to turn to G-d in
repentance. In Jewish Midrash, the trumpet-blowing in Ezekiel
thirty-three is speaking of Yom Teruah--the Day of the Blowing
of the Trumpet.[4] Remember that G-d made this a mo'ed. He has
an appointment to blow a shofar on this day.

The prophet Zephaniah, in the first chapter of his book,
speaks of the judgment coming on the land. At least twelve times
in the chapter, he refers to the Day of the L-rd, which has always

4) Kieval, Herman. The High Holy Days, (New York: The Burning Bush Press.,1959) pg. 98

Teshuvah 93

been interpreted by Rabbis as the Messianic Kingdom.[5] Knowing that Rosh haShanah is the set time (mo'ed) that the Day of the L-rd will begin, the frantic message of Elul is to repent of one's sins and return to G-d before the trumpet of Yom Teruah blows.

The scripture tells us that as the Messianic Kingdom begins, on earth there will be a cleansing of the altar. The Sabbath is a picture of the Messianic Kingdom, and in the days of the Temple, the priests began each Sabbath with a cleansing of the altar and the Temple.[6] So it will be in the Sabbath of G-d -- the Messianic Kingdom will begin with a cleansing. Sin will be dealt with among all the nations,[7] as G-d divides all men into two camps: one camp that rejects Him, and the other that believes in the G-d of Israel (through His Messiah). Because this will be the hardest period that the nation of Israel (as well as the other nations) will ever go through, the prophets labeled it the time of Jacob's Trouble:

> Alas! for that day is great, so that none is like it: it is even the time of Jacob's trouble, but he shall be saved out of it.
> Jeremiah 30:7

The Day (or Time) of Trouble referred to here is scattered throughout the Scriptures under various names: Birthpangs, Wrath of G-d, Tribulation, and so forth.[8] It describes a seven year time period of judgment and cleansing on the earth.[9]

The prophecy of the seventy weeks of Daniel 9.24-27 is understood to represent a 490 year period. Each week represents

5) See Appendix II

6) Edersheim, Alfred, The Temple, (Grand Rapids: Wm. B. Eerdmans Publishing Company., 1980), pgs. 181,187

7) Isa. 13.6-16; 24.1-23

8) See Appendix III

9) Dan. 9.27

seven years. An example from the Talmud showing a similar interpretation of the week is found in the following quote by Rabbi Simeon Ben Yohai:

> In the week when the son of David comes, in the first year this verse will be fulfilled: 'I will cause it to rain upon one city, and cause it not to rain upon another city.' In the second year the arrows of hunger will be sent forth. In the third a great famine; men, women, and children will die; pious men and saints (will be few), and the Law will be forgotten by its students. In the fourth, partial plenty. In the fifth, great plenty, when men will eat, drink and be merry, and the Law will return to its students. In the sixth, voices. In the seventh, war; and at the end of the seventh year, the son of David will come."
>
> Sanhedrin 97a

It is significant that Rabbi Simeon, whose prediction we find in the Talmud, is actually speaking of a seven-year tribulation period which will immediately precede the coming of the Messiah!

Rosh haShanah (Yom Teruah) teaches the beginning of Jacob's Trouble on earth[10] and the beginning of the Messianic Kingdom in heaven.[11] At the end of seven years, the Messiah returns to earth and rules from Jerusalem.[12] Because Yom Kippur is the appointment (mo'ed) for the Messiah to return to earth,[13] it is easily seen that the days between Rosh haShanah and Yom Kippur teach on the tribulation period, hence, the title

---

10) Joel 2.1; Isa. 18.3

11) Isa 26. 1-3; 57.1-2; I Thes. 4.13-18

12) Dan. 9.27; Zech 14; Isa. 2-4; Mic. 4.1-5

13) Isa. 52.13-15

"Yamim Nora-im" or "The Awesome Days".[14] This will be developed in a later chapter.

The forty-day period of Teshuvah can be divided into four sections:

(1) The thirty days of the month Elul.

(2) The day of Rosh haShanah.

(3) The days between Rosh haShanah and Yom Kippur.

(4) The day of Yom Kippur.

(1) The thirty days of Elul. The message is to repent of one's sins before Rosh haShanah and in so doing be inscribed in the Book of Life. The very greeting that is used among the Jewish people during Elul speaks of this: "May you be inscribed in the Book of Life." (The Book of The Wholly Righteous).[15] The people who are written in this book are not those who are righteous in themselves, but rather those who have received the Righteous One, the Messiah of Israel; for the prophet Isaiah said that our righteousness is not acceptable to G-d.[16]

> In those days, and at that time, will I cause the Branch of Righteousness to grow up unto David; and he shall execute judgment and righteousness in the land. In those days shall Judah be saved, and Jerusalem shall dwell safely: and this is his name wherewith she shall be called, THE L- RD OUR RIGHTEOUSNESS.
> Jeremiah 33.15-16

---

14) Joel 2.11

15) Rosh haShanah 16b

16) Isa. 64.6

Therefore, it is only through repentance of one's sins, and faith in the sacrificial death and resurrection of the Messiah, one is made righteous in the eyes of G-d and is written into the Book of Life.

In the overall scope of the plan of G-d, the world has come to the time of Elul.[17] The next appointment G-d will keep is the blowing of the shofar to announce the beginning of the Kingdom. Now is the time for the world to wake up and come to G-d. This is the time for a person to accept the Messiah. This and only this will allow someone to escape the judgment that is to come.

(2) The day of Rosh haShanah. This represents the beginning of the Messianic Kingdom. By this time the wise person has repented, for the judgment is now being passed. Those who have accepted the Messiah by this time, and are righteous, are immediately written and sealed in the Book of Life. Others have hardened their hearts against G-d. Their disastrous fate is sealed. The majority have not made a decision for or against G-d. Rosh haShanah is a final warning to them. They have ten days to return to G-d.

(3) The days between Rosh haShanah and Yom Kippur. This period reflects the seven-year period of Jacob's trouble. During this time, the greeting one uses changes to, "May you be sealed until the day of redemption" (Yom HaPeduth). Rav Shaul (Paul) referred to this expression with the same meaning used in this book in his letter to the Ephesians:

> And grieve not the Ruach haKodesh (the Holy Spirit) of G-d, whereby ye are sealed unto the day of redemption.
> Ephesians 4:30

(4) The day of Yom Kippur. This is the last division of the

---

17) See Epilogue

time of Teshuvah. It shows the second coming of the Messiah. It is the Day of Redemption (Yom HaPeduth). Realize that the forty-day period is designed by G-d to teach about His prophetic plan. This is related to the statement in Luke twenty-one that the generation who sees Jerusalem return to the Jews will also see the Messiah's second coming. In the Bible, a generation is 40 years (Hebrews three). This day-for-a-year equation was used by G-d in punishing Israel for its lack of faith to go into the promised land. They were sentenced to one year out of the land for each of the forty days that the spies had spent searching out the same land. We are in the generation Yeshua spoke of, as of June 7, 1967, when Jerusalem was taken from the hands of the Gentiles and given by G-d to Israel. The return of the Messiah is near. We are in the middle of the time of Teshuvah. May all who read this make a decision to repent of their sins and accept the Messiah.

At His second coming (Yom Kippur), Yeshua will reestablish His throne in Jerusalem, and all those who by faith have been gathered to Him will also reign with the Messiah for the remainder of the thousand years.[18] Those that are vessels fit for destruction and those intermediates who have not by this time received the Messiah will lose their life, eternally damned to Gehinnon.

18) Rev. 20.4

CHAPTER 8

THE DAY OF THE L-RD

The Day of the L-rd, referred to more than three hundred times within the scriptures (see Appendix II), is one of the major doctrines of the Bible. Its place is prominent in both the Tanach (Old Testament) as well as the New. In order to understand the overall message of the Bible and the role of the Messiah, it is necessary to see this event in its original intention.

The Bible's basic message is that of restoration. In creating the world, G-d made an environment that was perfect, and then placed man, also perfect, within it. Man had dominion over the earth, and was capable of performing the job; however, man sinned and became the servant of Nachash (the serpent).

> Know ye not, that to whom ye yield yourselves servants to obey, his servants ye are to whom ye obey; whether of sin unto death, or of obedience unto righteousness.
> Romans 6.16

According to the sages, if Adam had not sinned, he would have been immortal. However, because of sin, death entered the world -- not only death to man, but death of the earth itself, for it too was cursed. The Midrash on Genesis 2.4 speaks of the plan of restoration that G-d would initiate.

> These are the generations (toledot) of the heavens and of the earth when they were created, in the day that the L-rd G-d made the earth and the heavens.
> Genesis 2.4

In the above passage, "generations" or history is written in

Hebrew as "toledot." Note that this scripture precedes the fall of man in Genesis three. Following man's fall, the word is changed in its Hebrew spelling. From this point on, except for one passage to be discussed, one Hebrew letter is omitted from the original spelling of "toledot." This does not change the pronunciation of the word; but in the sages' mind, it did allude to something. In this they saw that man had been diminished by sin and had become mortal; therefore, the word used to represent the history of man had been diminished. The one other place that the word is spelled out in its complete form is in Ruth 4.18:

> Now these are the generations (toledot) of Pharez: Pharez begat Hezron.
>
> Ruth 4.18

This verse is seen as an allusion to the coming of the Messiah, who descends from Pharez. In Jewish liturgy, "the son of Peretz" is a title for the Messiah (see the song "L'chai Dodi"). The reason that the word "toledot" appears in its original spelling here is that with the coming of the Messiah "death will be swallowed up forever" (Isaiah 25.8).

A detailed explanation of the above is discussed in Me'am Lo'ez - *The Torah Anthology, Vol. 1,* by Rabbi Aryeh Kaplan, Maznaim Publishing Corporation, 1977, page 277.

For this reason, the Messiah is known as the "Redeemer" who comes to Zion. In Hebrew, the term for redeemer is "go'el." In ancient Israel society, when an individual had a debt or had lost his property or even his freedom because of his financial position, a close relative was called upon to redeem him from his debt. This relative was known as the "go'el." The go'el must meet two requirements: he must be the closest kin unless that right is passed to him, and he must be capable of paying the debt. According to Ibn Ezra, a famous rabbi, the redeemer or go'el of Isaiah fifty-nine is the Messiah as He comes to Zion having paid the debt for man.

The Messiah's task was to restore man to his former dominion, and the earth to its original perfection. Man was to become immortal, again in the image of G-d, living in the environment of Gan Eden (Garden of Eden).

The earth has gone through several phases that relate to the degeneration and restoration of man and the earth. The original phase was that existing before the fall of man. The second came about as a result of sin entering into the world. The heavens and the earth were changed, for now the curse was upon the earth. This phase would continue until the time of Noah's flood. In many ways both the earth and man were different from today. The earth was watered by a source underneath the face of the earth rather than by rain.

> And every plant of the field before it was in the earth, and every herb of the field before it grew: for the L-rd G-d had not caused it to rain upon the earth, and there was not a man to till the ground. But there went up a mist from the earth, and watered the whole face of the ground.
> Genesis 2.5-6

That this was the case at the time of Noah can be seen by the fact that until after the flood, G-d had not placed the rainbow in the sky, which is a natural by-product of rain. Secondly, the age of the people being so extremely long is understood by the great amount of water surrounding the earth before the flood.

> And G-d said, Let there be a firmament in the midst of the waters, and let it divide the waters from the waters. And G-d made the firmament, and divided the waters which were under the firmament from the waters which were above the firmament: and it was so. And G-d called the firmament Heaven. And the evening and the morning were the second day.
> Genesis 1.6-8

According to the account of the flood, there was enough water in the heavens to rain on the earth for forty days and nights. Our present atmospheric condition is incapable of producing rain for this length of time.

> In the six hundredth year of Noah's life in the second month, the seventeenth day of the month, the same day were all the fountains of the great deep broken up, and the windows of heaven were opened. And the rain was upon the earth forty days and forty nights.
>
> Genesis 7.11-12

Water in the atmosphere has been proved to be a deterrent to the aging rays of the sun. This is why, immediately following the flood, the life spans of mankind decreased rapidly.

With the flood, the earth and the heavens surrounding it changed. There was a new heaven and earth. This present heaven and earth will remain until the time of the Messianic Kingdom. This was spoken of by Shimon:

> For this they willingly are ignorant of, that by the word of G-d the heavens were of old, and the earth standing out of the water and in the water: whereby the world that then was, being overflowed with water, perished: But the heavens and the earth, which are now, by the same word are kept, in store reserved unto fire against the day of judgement and perdition of ungodly men.
>
> II Shimon (Peter) 3.5-7

There are yet two more scriptural phases of time described as "a new heaven and earth." One is when the Messianic Kingdom begins on earth, and the second is that which follows the Kingdom. Shimon (Peter) also spoke of the Messianic Kingdom "heaven and earth" in this chapter.

> But the day of the L-rd will come as a thief in the night; in the which the heavens shall pass away with a great noise, and the

elements shall melt with fervent heat, the earth also and the works that are therein shall be burned up. Seeing then that all these things shall be dissolved, what manner of persons ought ye to be in all holy conversation and godliness, looking for and hasting unto the coming of the day of G-d, wherein the heavens being on fire shall be dissolved, and the elements shall melt with fervent heat? Nevertheless we, according to His promise, look for new heavens and a new earth, wherein dwelleth righteousness.

Il Shimon (Peter) 3.10-13

The prophet Isaiah also spoke of this time.

For, behold, I create new heavens and a new earth: and the former shall not be remembered, nor come into mind. But be ye glad and rejoice for ever in that which I create: for, behold, I create Jerusalem a rejoicing, and her people a joy. And I will rejoice in Jerusalem, and joy in my people: and the voice of weeping shall be no more heard in her, nor the voice of crying. There shall be no more thence an infant of days, nor an old man that hath not filled his days: for the child shall die an hundred years old; but the sinner being a hundred years old shall be accursed. And they shall build houses, and inhabit them; and they shall plant vineyards, and eat the fruit of them. They shall not build, and another inhabit; they shall not plant, and another eat: for as the days of a tree are the days of my people, and mine elect shall long enjoy the work of their hands. They shall not labor in vain, nor bring forth for trouble; for they are the seed of the blessed of the L-rd, and their offspring with them. And it shall come to pass, that before they call, I will answer; and while they are yet speaking, I will hear. The wolf and the lamb shall feed together, and the lion shall eat straw like the bullock: and dust shall be the serpent's meat. They shall not hurt nor destroy in all my holy mountain, saith the L-rd.

Isaiah 65.17-25

In these two passages that deal with the Messianic Kingdom, known in Hebrew as the "Athid Lavo" (the coming age), several changes have taken place from our present world. The world is to have a great time of judgment ahead of it, but following that judgment, a time of peace and prosperity. The L-rd will make Jerusalem a place of rejoicing, instead of the place of frustration and violence that it is now. The extreme longevity of the people, reminiscent of the antediluvian period, returns. Even the nature of the animals will be altered; natural enemies cohabitate in peace. The carnivorous animals become vegetarians. Two things remain the same as today, however - sin and death.

It is important to note that the "new heaven and earth" are still this world. It is not that G-d is going to literally destroy this world with fire and replace it with another. Rather, a similar cataclysmic destruction such as Noah's flood will occur, with the outcome being an altered world. This can be established from a passage in Isaiah.

> In that day shall the Branch of the L-rd be beautiful and glorious, and the fruit of the earth shall be excellent and comely for them that are escaped of Israel. And it shall come to pass, that he that is left in Zion, and he that remaineth in Jerusalem, shall be called holy even everyone that is written among the living in Jerusalem: When the L-rd shall have washed away the filth of the daughters of Zion, and shall have purged the blood of Jerusalem from the midst thereof by the spirit of judgement, and by the spirit of burning.
>
> Isaiah 4.2-4

Following the end of the Messianic Kingdom, there will be the last "heaven and earth." This period is known as the "Olam Haba," which means "the world to come." Yochanan (John) spoke of this in the book of Revelation.

> And I saw a new heaven and a new earth: for the first heaven and the first earth were passed away; and there was no more sea. And I Yochanan saw the holy city, new Jerusalem, coming down from G-d out of heaven, prepared as a bride adorned for her husband. And I heard a great voice out of heaven saying, Behold the tabernacle of G-d is with men, and He will dwell with

them, and they shall be His people, and G-d Himself shall be with them, and be their G-d. And G-d shall wipe away all tears from their eyes; and there shall be no more death, neither sorrow, nor crying, neither shall there be any more pain: for the former things are passed away.

Revelation 21.1-4

By comparing this passage with the previous one from Isaiah that deals with the Messianic Kingdom, several differences come to light. In the latter "heaven and earth," there is no death, no sorrow, and obviously no sin. This is the final restoration.

There is a parallel between the Messianic Kingdom and the period from the fall until the flood. Besides the life span being extended in each, the earth is described as returning to a near Garden of Eden state.

And it shall come to pass in that day, that the mountains shall drop down new wine, and the hills shall flow with milk, and all the rivers of Judah shall flow with waters, and a fountain shall come of the House of the L-rd, and shall water the valley of Shittim.

Joel 3.18

The reader might have observed that the restoration of the world seems to be going in a circle. First there was the magnificent creation, then the world from the garden till the flood, then the present age, soon to be replaced by the Messianic Kingdom, followed by the Olam Haba, which brings us back to the state of the world before the fall.

This restoration is spoken of by Shimon (Peter) in the book of Acts.

And He shall send Yeshua the Messiah, which before was preached unto you: whom the heaven must receive until the times of restitution of all things, which G-d hath spoken by the mouth of all his holy prophets since the world began.

Acts 3.20-21

The Day of the L-rd   **105**

This "restoration" was called the "basar," which means "good news," and is commonly known as the "gospel." Hundreds of years before the Messiah's birth in Bethlehem, the "basar" was well known and well defined; every Jewish child was reared on these precepts. The "basar" was not the Messiah, rather the Messiah was the agent of the "basar." This "good news" contained the following: the universal reign of G-d, the reestablishment of the House of David, the future glory of an Israel returned to G-d, the ingathering of the exiles, the resurrection of the dead, and the reward and punishment in the last judgment.

The eschatological hope of the Jewish people was expressed in terms that denoted the kingship of G-d. His throne was said to be coming to earth. This is not to deny that G-d has always been on the throne in Jewish theology, nor that such men as Abraham and David were not under His dominion. It was understood that before the fall, the "Kingdom of G-d" was over the entire earth with Adam as the earthly ruler under G-d. The redemption of man and earth would restore that throne to its rightful place.

The term "Kingdom of G-d" was replaced by one of its synonyms "Kingdom of Heaven," called the "Malkut Shamayim" in Hebrew. Therefore, the "habasar haMalkut Shamayim" or the "Gospel of the Kingdom of Heaven" is a phrase that every Jew of the first century understood, and included many expectations long established before that time. Hundreds of years before the time of Yeshua the prophet Isaiah had written:

> O Zion, that bringest good tidings (the basar), get thee up into the high mountain; O Jerusalem, that bringest good tidings (basar), lift up thy voice with strength; lift it up, be not afraid; say unto the cities of Judah, Behold your G-d! Behold the L-rd G-d will come with strong hand, and His arm shall rule for Him: behold, His reward is with Him, and His work before Him. He shall feed His flock like a shepherd: He shall gather the lambs

with His arm, and carry them in His bosom, and shall gently lead those that are with young.
Isaiah 40.9-11

It is with this background that Yeshua began His ministry.

Now after that Yochanan was put in prison, Yeshua came into Galilee, preaching the gospel (basar) of the Kingdom of G-d (Heaven), and saying, The time is fulfilled, and the Kingdom of G-d (Heaven) is at hand (present): repent ye and believe the gospel (basar).
Mark 1.14-15

The "Malkut Shamayim" or "Kingdom of Heaven" is the end result of the "good news" of the restoration. Several questions arise concerning the first coming of the Messiah. If the gospel was defined as the ingathering of the exiles, the universal reign of G-d over the entire earth, the reestablishment of the house of David, et cetera, then did Yeshua fulfill the Gospel? The answer is that with Yeshua's coming, the restoration began and will be completed in the second coming.

For more than four hundred years before the time of Yeshua, and dating back to the days of Zechariah and Habakkuk, there had not been anyone upon which the Spirit of G-d had rested. This period is known as the four hundred silent years. In Jewish expectation the next prophet to come on the scene would be Elijah, who would precede the Messiah. With Elijah's coming, prophesy would be restored to Israel. In the first coming, Yeshua received the anointing of the Ruach haKodesh (the Holy Spirit). With this event, He received the power of the Spirit of the Father, which was an initial step in the restoration.

Behold my servant, whom I uphold; mine elect, in whom my soul delighteth; I have put My Ruach (Spirit) upon Him: he shall bring forth judgement to the Gentiles.
Isaiah 42.1

> Now when all the people were immersed, it came to pass, that
> Yeshua also being immersed, and praying, the heaven was
> opened, and the Ruach haKodesh (the Holy Spirit) descended
> in a bodily shape like a dove upon Him, and a voice came from
> heaven, which said, Thou art My beloved Son; in Thee I am well
> pleased.
>
> Luke 3.21-22

This power was the same power that Adam had held before his fall (see Hebrews 6.5 where this power is equated to the power of "the world to come"). Yeshua healed the sick, cast out demons, et cetera; all of these being events of restoration and promises of the future Day of the L-rd. He was the first to die and experience the full restoration into the glorified body that Adam had. By His death, He conquered sin, and defeated death. The redemption was performed in His sacrifice. Therefore, Yeshua was the first to experience the restoration, thereby opening the way for this same restoration to be delivered to those who believe in Him.

> And the Redeemer shall come to Zion, and unto them that turn
> from transgression in Jacob, saith the L-rd. As for me, this is my
> covenant with them, saith the L-rd; My Spirit that is upon thee,
> and my words which I have put in thy mouth, shall not depart
> out of thy mouth, nor out of the mouth of thy seed, nor out of thy
> seed's seed, saith the L-rd, from henceforth and for ever.
>
> Isaiah 59.20-21

> In the last day, that great day of the feast, Yeshua stood and
> cried, saying, If any man thirst, let him come unto me, and drink.
> He that believeth on me, as the Scripture hath said, out of his
> belly shall flow rivers of living water. But this spake He of the
> Ruach (Spirit), which they that believe on Him should receive:
> for the Ruach haKodesh (the Holy Spirit) was not yet given;
> because that Yeshua was not yet glorified.
>
> Yochanan (John) 7.37-39

Fifty days following the resurrection of Yeshua, the Kingdom was delivered to the believers, evidenced by the outpouring of the Spirit upon the believers at Shavuot (Pentecost).

> And when the day of Shavuot (Pentecost) was fully come, they were all with one accord in one place. And suddenly there came a sound from heaven as of a rushing mighty wind, and it filled all the house where they were sitting. And there appeared unto them cloven tongues like as of fire, and it sat upon each of them. And they were all filled with the Ruach haKodesh (the Holy Spirit), and began to speak with other tongues, as the Ruach (Spirit) gave them utterance.
>
> Acts 2.1-4

With this, the believers entered into the restoration, but it was only a partial restoration with a promise of more to come. As Yeshua had received a new body, so too would those who believe in Yeshua. This resurrection occurs with Messiah's return. The second coming is the advent of the Day of the L-rd.

The Day of the L-rd is complex in its makeup, because several different programs of G-d are going on at the same time. On the first day of the period known as the Day of the L-rd, the Shofar will sound; the resurrection of the righteous, as well as the catching away of all the believers alive at that time, will occur. They receive their glorified bodies. They will be gathered for the Coronation of Yeshua and the Marriage of the Messiah to His bride; all of this is to be the six thousandth Rosh haShanah since the creation. On earth, those who are not caught away will be thrown into the "time of trouble," most commonly known as the "birthpangs of the Messiah," but also called the "wrath of G-d," "tribulation," and "indignation" (see Appendix III). During this time, the earth will be purged from sin.

> Behold, the day of the L-rd cometh, cruel both with wrath and fierce anger, to lay the land desolate: and He shall destroy the sinners thereof out of it. For the stars of heaven and the constellations thereof shall not give their light: the sun shall be

darkened in his going forth, and the moon shall not cause her light to shine. And I will punish the world for their evil, and the wicked for their iniquity; and I will cause the arrogancy of the proud to cease, and will lay low the haughtiness of the terrible. I will make a man more precious than fine gold; even a man than the golden wedge of Ophir. Therefore I will shake the heavens, and the earth shall remove out of her place, in the wrath of the L-rd of hosts, and in the day of His fierce anger.

Isaiah 13.9-13

And it shall come to pass, that in all the land, saith the L-rd, two parts therein shall be cut off and die; but the third shall be left therein. And I will bring the third part through the fire, and will refine them as silver is refined, and will try them as gold is tried: they shall call on my name, and I will hear them: I will say, It is my people: and they shall say, The L-rd is my G-d.

Zechariah 13.8-9

Many will turn to the G-d of heaven through the Messiah, while others harden their hearts. At the end of the seven years, Yeshua will come to Jerusalem, destroying the enemies that have come against her.

Who is this that cometh from Edom, with dyed garments from Bozrah? this that is glorious in His apparel, traveling in the greatness of His strength? I that speak in righteousness, mighty to save. Wherefore art Thou red in Thine apparel, and thy garments like him that treadeth in the winevat? I have trodden the winepress alone; and of the people there was none with Me: for I will tread them in Mine anger, and trample them in My fury; and their blood shall be sprinkled upon my garments, and I will stain all my raiment. For the day of vengeance is in mine heart, and the year of My redeemed is come. And I looked, and there was none to help; and I wondered that there was none to uphold: therefore Mine Own arm brought salvation unto Me; and My fury, it upheld Me. And I will tread down the people in Mine anger, and make them drunk in My fury, and I will bring down their strength to the earth.

Isaiah 63.1-6

Behold the day of the L-rd cometh, and thy spoil shall be divided in the midst of thee. For I will gather all nations against Jerusalem to battle; and the city shall be taken, and the houses rifled, and the women ravished; and half of the city shall go forth into captivity, and the residue of the people shall not be cut off from the city. Then shall the L-rd go forth, and fight against those nations, as when He fought in the day of battle. And His feet shall stand in that day upon the mount of Olives, which is before Jerusalem on the east, and the mount of Olives shall cleave in the midst thereof toward the east and toward the west, and there shall be a very great valley; and half of the mountain shall remove toward the north, and half of it toward the south. And ye shall flee to the valley of the mountains; for the valley of the mountains shall reach unto Azal: yea, ye shall flee, like as ye fled from before the earthquake in the days of Uzziah king of Judah: and the L-rd my G-d shall come, and all the saints with Thee. And it shall come to pass in that day, that the light shall not be clear, nor dark: but it shall be one day which shall be known to the L-rd, not day, nor night: but it shall come to pass, that at evening time it shall be light. And it shall be in that day that living waters shall go out from Jerusalem; half of them toward the former sea, and half of them toward the hinder sea: in summer and winter shall it be. And the L-rd shall be king over all the earth: in that day shall there be one L-rd, and His name one.
Zechariah 14.1-9

With Messiah's return, the reign of peace, and ingathering of exiles will arrive.

And there shall come forth a rod out of the stem of Jesse, and a Branch shall grow out of His roots: and the spirit of the L-rd shall rest upon Him, the spirit of wisdom and understanding, the spirit of counsel and might, the spirit of knowledge and of the fear of the L-rd; and shall make Him of quick understanding in the fear of the L-rd. And He shall not judge after the sight of His eyes, neither reprove after the hearing of His ears: but with righteousness shall He judge the poor, and reprove with equity for the meek of the earth: and He shall smite the earth with the rod of His mouth, and with the breath of His lips shall He slay the wicked. And righteousness shall be the girdle of His loins and faithfulness the girdle of His reins. The wolf also shall dwell with the lamb, and the leopard shall lie down with the kid; and the calf and the young lion and the fatling together; and a little child shall lead them. and the cow and the bear shall feed; their young ones shall lie down together: and the lion shall eat straw like the ox. And the sucking child shall play on the hole of the asp, and the weaned child shall put his hand on the cockatrice den. They shall not hurt nor destroy in all My holy mountain: for the earth shall be full of the knowledge of the L-rd, as the waters cover the sea. And in that day there shall be a root of Jesse, which shall stand for an ensign of the people; to it shall the Gentiles seek: and His rest shall be glorious. And it shall come to pass in that day, that the L- rd shall set His hand again the second time to recover the remnant of His people, which shall be left, from Assyria, and from Egypt, and from Pathros, and from Cush, and from Elam, and from Shinar, and from Hamath, and from the islands of the sea. and He shall set up an ensign for the nations, and shall assemble the outcasts of Israel, and gather together the dispersed of Judah from the four corners of the earth.

Isaiah 11.1-12

Thus, the House of David will be reestablished in the golden age of Israel. Those who died during the "birthpangs" and became believers in the Messiah will receive their glorified bodies and join the others reigning over the earth. Two types of people will inhabit the earth - those in resurrected bodies, and those who became believers during the "birthpangs," who did not die.

And I saw thrones, and they sat upon them, and judgement was given unto them: and I saw the souls of them that were beheaded for the witness of Yeshua, and for the word of G-d, and which had not worshipped the beast, neither his image, neither had received his mark upon their foreheads, or in their hands; and they lived and reigned with Messiah a thousand years. But the rest of the dead lived not again until the thousand years were finished. This is the first resurrection. Blessed and holy is he that hath part in the first resurrection: on such the second death hath no power, but they shall be priests of G-d and of Messiah, and shall reign with Him a thousand years.

Revelation 20.4-6

This last group will be gathered to Jerusalem, their tears wiped away, their diseases healed, and the Ruach (Spirit) poured out upon them.

Until the Ruach (Spirit) be poured upon us from on high, and the wilderness be a fruitful field, and the fruitful field be counted for a forest. Then judgement shall dwell in the wilderness, and righteousness remain in the fruitful field. And the work of righteousness shall be peace; and the effect of righteousness, quietness and assurance for ever. And My people shall dwell in a peaceable habitation, and in sure dwellings, and in quiet resting places; when it shall hail, coming down on the forest; and the city shall be low in a low place. Blessed are ye that sow beside all waters, that send forth thither the feet of the ox and the ass.

Isaiah 32.15-20

At the end of the thousand years, Satan will have his last rebellion, gathering those who rejected the Messiah during the Kingdom Age (some of the descendants of the believers who survived the "birthpangs"). Messiah will crush this rebellion and then judge all who rejected Him from all time.

And when the thousand years are expired, Satan shall be loosed out of his prison, and shall go out to deceive the nations which are in the four quarters of the earth, Gog and Magog, to gather them together to battle: the number of whom is as the sand of the sea. And they went up on the breadth of the earth, and encompassed the camp of the saints about, and the beloved city: and fire came down from G-d out of heaven, and devoured them. And the devil that deceived them was cast into the lake of fire and brimstone, where the beast and the false prophet are, and shall be tormented day and night for ever and ever. And I saw a great white throne, and Him that sat on it, from whose face the earth and the heaven fled away; and there was found no

place for them. And I saw the dead, small and great, stand before
G-d; and the books were opened: and another book was
opened, which is the book of life: and the dead were judged out
of those things which were written in the books, according to
their works. And the sea gave up the dead which were in it; and
death and hell delivered up the dead which were in them: and
they were judged every man according to their works. And death
and hell were cast into the lake of fire. This is the second death.
And whosoever was not found written in the book of life was cast
into the lake of fire.

Revelation 20.7-15

Along with the judgment of those who rejected the Messiah,
all of those who accepted and lived during the thousand years now
receive their glorified bodies. The kingdom period will be at an
end and now be turned over to the Father, for the "Olam Haba,"
the "World to Come." The restoration is now complete.

Then cometh the end, when He shall have delivered up the
kingdom to G-d, even the Father; when He shall have put down
all rule, and all authority and power. For He must reign, till He
hath put all enemies under His feet. The last enemy that shall be
destroyed is death. For He hath put all things under His feet. But
when He saith, All things are put under Him, it is manifest that
He is excepted, which did put all things under Him. And when
all things shall be subdued unto Him, then shall the Son also
Himself be subject unto Him that put all things under Him, that
G-d may be all in all.

I Corinthians 15.24-28

CHAPTER 9

TWO THEATERS

A problem exists concerning Rosh haShanah. As the Messianic prophecies often presented a paradox (Suffering Servant/Conquering King), so do the themes of Rosh haShanah. It seems impossible that the Messianic Kingdom, which is to be a one thousand-year reign of peace, could begin with the time of Jacob's trouble, with all its war, death, and destruction. The answer is found in two theaters of operation. One is on earth, where the birthpangs of the Messiah (tribulation) will be happening. The other is in heaven during the same seven-year period. As mentioned previously, Rosh haShanah is also Yom haDin, the Day of Judgment. On this day all mankind pass before G-d and are divided into three categories.

> Said Rabbi Krusvedai in the name of Rabbi Yochanan: Three books are opened on Rosh haShanah: one for the wholly righteous, one for the wholly wicked and one for the intermediates. The wholly righteous are at once inscribed and sealed in the Book of Life; the wholly wicked are at once inscribed and sealed in the Book of Death; and the intermediates are held suspended from Rosh haShanah until Yom Kippur. If they are found worthy, they are inscribed for life; if found unworthy, they are inscribed for death.
>
> Rosh haShanah 16b, version of En Yaakov

The first category is that of the wholly righteous. In this category are all those who by faith in the Messiah have received the righteousness of G-d. They are known as the Tzadikim or saints. If you are a believer in Yeshua, then you belong to this group. Those believers who are alive at the end of six thousand years, the beginning of the seventh day or the Messianic kingdom, will be separated to G-d and totally removed from entering the cleansing period in the theater on earth.

> Neither their silver nor their gold shall be able to deliver them in the day of the L-rd's wrath; but the whole land shall be devoured by the fire of His jealousy: for he shall make even a speedy riddance of all them that dwell in the land. Gather yourselves together, yea, gather together, O nation not desired; before the decree bring forth, before the day pass as the chaff, before the fierce anger of the L-rd come upon you, before the day of the L-rd's anger come upon you. Seek ye the L-rd, all ye meek of the earth, which have wrought his judgment; seek righteousness, seek meekness: it may be ye shall be hid in the day of the L-rd's anger.
> Zephaniah 1.18-2.3

Note in the above passage that those who have received the righteousness of G-d before the Day of the L-rd begins are expecting to be hidden from the wrath of G-d. Another example of the righteous being hidden from the wrath of G-d is found in Psalm 27.5, which is read daily during the season of Teshuvah.

> For in the time of trouble (Jacob's trouble) He shall hide me in His pavilion: in the secret of his tabernacle shall He hide me; He shall set me up upon a rock.
> Psalm 27.5

When the following two passages are superimposed, they yield a complete picture. Note that the righteous are taken away from the evil and enter into peace. The gates are opened to let them enter. In Judaism, the gates of heaven are opened during the Mussaf service of Rosh haShanah. Likewise, they are closed at the conclusion of the Neilah service of Yom Kippur.[1] Thus,

---

1) Isa. 26.1-3; Psa. twenty-four

they enjoy the benefits of peace and joy in the heavenly theater while the earth is experiencing harsh judgment.

The righteous perisheth, and no man layeth it to heart: and merciful men are taken away, none considering that the righteous is taken away from the evil to come. He shall enter into peace: they shall rest in their beds, each one walking in his uprightness.

Isaiah 57.1,2

In that day (the Day of the L-rd) shall this song be sung in the land of Judah; We have a strong city; salvation will G-d appoint for walls and bulwarks. Open ye the gates, that the righteous nation which keepeth the truth may enter in. Thou wilt keep him in perfect peace, whose mind is stayed on thee: because he trusteth in thee.

Isaiah 26.1-3

As the shofar sounds inaugurating the last day, not only those living Tzadikim, but also those who have died believing in the Messiah will be gathered to Him.

Thy dead men shall live, together with my dead body shall they arise. Awake and sing, ye that dwell in dust: for thy dew is as the dew of herbs, and the earth shall cast out the dead. Come my people, enter thou into thy chambers, and shut thy doors about thee: hide thyself as it were for a little moment, until the indignation be over-passed. For, behold, the L-rd cometh out of His place to punish the inhabitants of the earth for their iniquity: the earth also shall disclose her blood and shall no more cover her slain.

Isaiah 26.19-21

But I would not have you to be ignorant, brethren, concerning them which are asleep, that ye sorrow not, even as others which have no hope. For if we believe that Yeshua died and rose again, even so them also which sleep in Yeshua will G-d bring with Him. For this we say unto you by the word of the L-rd, that we which are alive and remain until the coming of the L-rd shall not prevent them which are asleep. For the L-rd Himself shall descend from heaven with a shout, with the voice of the archangel, and with the trumpet of G-d: and the dead in Messiah will rise first: then we which are alive and remain shall be caught up together with them in the clouds, to meet the L-rd in the air: and so shall we ever be with the L-rd. Wherefore comfort one another with these words. But of the times and the seasons, brethren, ye have no need that I write unto you. For yourselves know perfectly that the Day of the L-rd so cometh as a thief in the night. For when they shall say, Peace and safety; then sudden destruction cometh upon them, as travail upon a woman with child; and they shall not escape.

I Thessalonians 4.13-5.3

The next several chapters concerning the wedding and coronation will deal in detail with what should be expected by the believers in this theater in heaven.

The other theater on earth is one of a totally different nature. It contains the other two categories: the Rashim or wicked (vessels fit for destruction) and the middling class (average people). The quote from Rabbi Yochanan shows the concept that the vessels fit for destruction are sealed for death on Rosh haShanah, but the average people (middling class) are given until Yom Kippur to repent. For these two groups indeed the days will be awesome.

Blow ye the trumpet in Zion, and sound an alarm in my holy mountain: let all the inhabitants of the land tremble: for the day of the L-rd cometh, for it is nigh at hand. For the day of the L-rd is great and very terrible [nora--awesome], and who can abide it.

Joel 2.1,11b

The great day of the L-rd is near, it is near, and hasteth greatly, even the voice of the day of the L-rd: the mighty man shall cry there bitterly. That day is a day of wrath, a day of trouble and distress, a day of wasteness and desolation, a day of darkness and gloominess, a day of clouds and thick darkness, a day of the trumpet and alarm against the fenced cities and against the high towers. And I will bring distress upon men, that they shall walk like blind men, because they have sinned against the L-rd: and their blood shall be poured out as dust, and their flesh as the dung.

Zephaniah 1.14-17

Come near, ye nations to hear; and hearken, ye people: let the earth hear and all that is therein; the world, and all things that come forth of it. For the indignation of the L-rd is upon all nations, and his fury upon all their armies: he hath utterly destroyed them, he hath delivered them to the slaughter. Their slain also shall be cast out, and their stink shall come up out of their carcasses, and the mountains shall be melted with their blood. And all the host of heaven shall be dissolved, and the heavens shall be rolled together as a scroll: and all their host shall fall down, as the leaf falleth off from the vine, and as a falling fig from the fig tree. For it is the day of the L-rd's vengeance and the year of recompenses for the controversy of Zion.

Isaiah 34.1-4,8

And the heaven departed as a scroll when it is rolled together; and every mountain and island were moved out of their places. And the kings of the earth, and the great men, and the rich men, and the chief captains, and the mighty men, and every bondman, and every freeman, hid themselves in the dens and in the rocks of the mountains; and said to the mountains and rocks, Fall on us, and hide us from the face of him that sitteth on the throne and from the wrath of the Lamb: for the great day of his wrath is come; and who shall be able to stand?

Revelation 6.14-17

This is why the days between Rosh haShanah and Yom Kippur are called Yamim Nora'im--the Awesome Days. This same time period is often called the Day of the Wrath of G-d, the Indignation, Jacob's Trouble, or the Birthpangs of the Messiah.

The "Birthpangs of Messiah," an idiom that is used

throughout Rabbinic literature, has been drawn from numerous passages of Scripture.[2] It is linked to the time of trouble and the Day of the L-rd. Note Rav Shaul's (Paul's) use of it in I Thessalonians 4.13-5.3 (already quoted).

> And these are the words that the L-rd spake concerning Israel and concerning Judah. For thus saith the L-rd; we have heard a voice of trembling, of fear, and not of peace. Ask ye now, and see whether a man doth travail with child? Wherefore do I see every man with his hands on his loins, as a woman in travail, and all faces are turned into paleness? Alas! for that day is great, so that none is like it: it is even the time of Jacob's trouble; but he shall be saved out of it.
>
> Jeremiah 30.4-7

> Howl ye; for the day of the L-rd is at hand; it shall come as a destruction from the Almighty. Therefore shall all hands be faint, and every man's heart shall melt: and they shall be afraid: pangs and sorrows shall take hold of them; they shall be in pain as a woman that travaileth: they shall be amazed one at another; their faces shall be as flames. Behold, the day of the L-rd cometh, cruel both with wrath and fierce anger, to lay the land desolate: and he shall destroy the sinners thereof out of it.
>
> Isaiah 13.6-9

> L-rd, in trouble have they visited thee, they poured out a prayer when thy chastening was upon them. Like as a woman with child that draweth near the time of her delivery, is in pain, and crieth out in her pangs; so have we been in thy sight, O L-rd.
>
> Isaiah 26.16,17

> But thou, Bethlehem Ephratah, though thou be little among the thousands of Judah, yet out of thee shall he [Messiah] come forth unto me that is to be ruler in Israel; whose goings forth have been from of old, from everlasting. Therefore, will he give them up, until the time that she which travaileth hath brought forth:

---

2)   See Appendix III

then the remnant of his brethren shall return unto the children of Israel.

Micah 5.2,3

And there appeared a great wonder in heaven; a woman [Israel] clothed with the sun, the moon under her feet, and upon her head a crown of twelve stars: and she being with child cried, travailing in birth, and pained to be delivered. And she brought forth a man child, who was to rule all nations with a rod of iron: and her child was caught up unto G-d, unto his throne.

Revelation 12.1,2,5

Before she travailed, she brought forth: before her pain came, she was delivered of a man child. Who hath heard such a thing? Who hath seen such things? Shall the earth be made to bring forth in one day? Or shall a nation be born at once? For as soon as Zion travailed, she brought forth her children.

Isaiah 66.7,8

George Foot-Moore, in his work *Judaism in the First Century Christian Era*, correctly defines the birthpangs as follows:

"It was evidently expected that these 'pangs' would be understood of the travail in which the new age was to be born. The corresponding phrase in the Rabbinical text is 'the travail of the Messiah,' that is, not the sufferings of the Messiah himself, as it has sometimes been erroneously explained, but the throes of mother Zion which is in labor to bring forth the Messiah without metaphor, the Jewish people."[3]

Understand that it is not the Messiah who is born, but rather Israel as a corporate nation that is accepting her Messiah, i. e., being born anew spiritually. What an appropriate analogy G-d chose in this idiom to portray the struggles, pains, but glorious results of this time period in the theater of earth.

---

3) Foote-Moore, George, <u>Judaism in the First Century Christian Era</u>, (Cambridge: Harvard University Press., 1927), Part V. pg. 361

Yeshua, when asked about his second coming, spoke of the tribulation period as beginning with the birthpangs:

> And as he sat upon the Mount of Olives, the disciples came unto him privately, saying, Tell us, when shall these things be? and what shall be the sign of thy coming, and of the end of the world? And Yeshua answered and said unto them, Take heed that no man deceive you, for many shall come in my name, saying, I am Messiah; and shall deceive many. And ye shall hear of wars and rumors of wars: see that ye be not troubled: for all these things must come to pass, but the end is not yet. For nation shall rise against nation, and kingdom against kingdom: and there shall be famines, and pestilences, and earthquakes in diverse places. All these are the beginning of sorrows (birthpangs).
>
> Mattatiyahu (Matthew) 24.3-8

Indeed, this time will be the most horrible time mankind has ever witnessed. Even the Nazi holocaust of World War II cannot compare to the pain of this period. G-d is coming forth to judge sin and every nation. In the midst of this, many of the average people, who waited until now, will turn to G-d and call upon His Messiah for deliverance. An evil ruler, the false messiah, will arise in the world and proclaim that he is G-d.

> Let no man deceive you by any means: for that day shall not come, except there come a falling away first, and that man of sin be revealed, the son of perdition; who opposeth and exalteth himself above all that is called G-d, or that is worshipped: so that he as G-d sitteth in the Temple of G-d, showing himself that he is G-d. Even him, whose coming is after the working of Satan with all power and signs and lying wonders and with all deceivableness of unrighteousness in them that perish; because they receive not the love of truth that they might be saved. And for this cause G-d shall send them strong delusion, that they should believe a lie: that they all might be damned who believed not the truth, but had pleasure in unrighteousness.
>
> II Thessalonians 2.3,4,9-12

This false messiah will make war against these new saints and

will prevail against them until the legitimate Messiah comes
again.

And the ten horns which thou sawest are ten kings, which have
received no kingdom as yet; but receive power as kings one hour
with the beast. These have one mind, and shall give their power
and strength unto the beast. These shall make war with the
Lamb, and the Lamb shall overcome them, for he is L-rd of lords
and King of kings: and they that are with him are called, and
chosen, and faithful.
Revelation 17,12-14

Then I would know the truth of the fourth beast, which was
diverse from all the others, exceeding dreadful, whose teeth
were of iron, and his nails of brass; which devoured, brake in
pieces, and stamped the residue with his feet; and of the ten
horns that were in his head, and of the other which came up, and
before whom three fell; even of that horn that had eyes, and a
mouth that spake very great things, whose look was more stout
than his fellows. I beheld, and the same horn made war with the
saints and prevailed against them; until the Ancient of Days
came, and judgment was given to the saints of the Most High
and the time that the saints possessed the kingdom.
Daniel 7.19-22

Yeshua's return, consistent with the teachings of Yom
Kippur, will be at the end of the seventh year, almost assuredly
on a Yom Kippur. A description of Messiah's return is seen in
Isaiah fifty-two, where just as the high priest sprinkled the people
for cleansing on Yom Kippur,[4] Yeshua will sprinkle the nations.

Behold, my servant shall deal prudently, he shall be exalted and
extolled, and be very high. As many were astonished at thee: his
visage was so marred more than any man, and his form more
than the sons of men: So shall he sprinkle many nations; the
kings shall shut their mouths at him: for that which had not been

---

4) Lev. sixteen

Two Theaters

told them shall they see; and that which they had not heard shall
they consider.

Isaiah 52.13-15

The ceremony that closes the Yom Kippur service, Neilah, is
also brought out in Messiah's second coming. Neilah, meaning
the "closing of the gate," communicates the message to all of those
that have not yet repented, that there comes a point when it is too
late to accept the Messiah. During this service a shofar called the
Great Shofar (Shofar haGadol) is blown just before the gate is
finally closed. Even so, at Messiah's coming the Shofar haGadol
will be blown, the gates closed, and all gathered to Jerusalem.

Immediately after the tribulation of those days shall the sun be
darkened, and the moon shall not give her light, and the stars
shall fall from heaven, and the powers of the heavens shall be
shaken: and then shall appear the sign of the Son of man in
heaven: and then shall all the tribes of the earth mourn, and they
shall see the Son of man coming in the clouds of heaven with
power and great glory. And He shall send his angels with a great
sound of a trumpet (Shofar HaGadol), and they shall gather
together his elect from the four winds, from one end of heaven
to the other.

Mattatiyahu (Matthew) 24:29-31

And it shall come to pass in that Day, that the L-rd shall beat off
from the channel of the river unto the stream of Egypt, and ye
shall be gathered one by one, O ye children of Israel. And it shall
come to pass in that Day, that the great trumpet (Shofar
HaGadol) shall be blown, and they shall come which were ready
to perish in the land of Assyria, and the outcasts in the land of
Egypt, and shall worship the L-rd in the holy mount at Jerusalem.

Isaiah 27:12-13

Those who believed and survived the terrible days in the
theater on earth will be in a time period for which all creation has
waited six millennia.

In that day shall the branch of the L-rd be beautiful and glorious, and the fruit of the earth shall be excellent and comely from them that are escaped of Israel. And it shall come to pass, that he that is left in Zion, and he that remaineth in Jerusalem, shall be called holy, even everyone that is written among the living in Jerusalem: when the L-rd shall have washed away the filth of the daughters of Zion, and shall have purged the blood of Jerusalem from the midst thereof by the spirit of judgment, and by the spirit of burning. And the L-rd will create upon every dwelling place of Mt. Zion, and upon her assemblies, a cloud and smoke by day, and the shining of a flaming fire by night: for upon all the glory shall be a defense. And there shall be a tabernacle for a shadow in the daytime from the heat, and for a place of refuge, and for a covert from storm and from rain.

Isaiah 4.2-6

What the reader should keep in mind is that the beginning of the Messianic Kingdom will be a time of peace and comfort, but it will also be a time of calamity and disaster, depending on which theater one finds himself in. This should also clear up any doubts one might have regarding what the Bible says concerning the time period of the tribulation.

The Natzal and Ressurection

CHAPTER 10

THE NATZAL AND RESURRECTION

Within the confines of Jewish belief, faith in the Messiah and the resurrection of the dead go hand in hand. Without the resurrection, there is no belief in the Messiah and vice versa. In Rabbinic literature, the belief in the resurrection in the Messianic days became a basic tenet. On that basis, the belief in the resurrection was among the Thirteen Articles of Faith of Maimonides.

I believe with a perfect faith that there will be a resurrection of the dead at a time when the will shall arise from the Creator, may His Name be blessed and His remembrance exalted for all eternity.

Maimonides, Thirteen Articles of the Faith, Article 13

And at that time shall Michael stand up, the great prince which standeth for the children of thy people: and there shall be a time of trouble, such as never was since there was a nation even to that same time: and at that time thy people shall be delivered, everyone that shall be found written in the book. And many of them that who sleep in the dust of the earth shall awake, some to everlasting life and some to shame and everlasting contempt. And they that be wise shall shine as the brightness of the firmament; and they that turn many to righteousness as the stars for ever and ever.

Daniel 12.1-3

Not only in the scriptures, but throughout the liturgical prayers, midrashim, apocrypha, and targumim the faith in the resurrection at the advent of the Messianic Kingdom was expressed.

In that hour the Holy one, blessed be He, will crown the Messiah and place a helmet of salvation on his head, and give him splendor and radiance, and adorn him with clothes of honor, and stand him up on top of a high mountain in order to bring glad tidings to Israel. And he will let it be heard with his voice: "Salvation is near!" And Israel will say: "Who are you?" And he will say: "I am Ephraim." And Israel will say: "Are you the one whom the Holy One, blessed be He, called 'Ephraim My firstborn, Ephraim is a darling son to Me'?" and he will say, "Yes." And Israel will say to him: "Go and bring glad tidings to them that sleep in [the Cave of] Machpela, that they should rise first."

In that hour he goes up and brings glad tidings to those who sleep in Machpela, and says to them: "Abraham, Isaac, and Jacob, rise! Enough have you slept!" And they reply and say: "Who is this who removes the dust from over us?" And he says to them: "I am the Messiah of the L-rd. Salvation is near, the hour is near." And they answer: "If it really is so, go and bring the tidings to Adam the first man, so that he should rise first." In that hour they say to Adam the first man: "Enough have you slept." And he says: "Who is this who drives the slumber from my eyes?" And he says: "I am the Messiah of G-d, from among the children of your children." Instantly Adam the first man and all his generation, and Abraham, Isaac, and Jacob, and all the pious and all the tribes and all the generations from one end of the world to the other rise and utter sounds of jubilation and song....And how beautiful are Moses and his generation coming from the desert!

This can be likened to a king who had two sons, and one of them died, and all the people of the country put on black garments. The king said: "You put on black garments now when my first son died; I shall dress you in white for the rejoicing [the wedding] of my second son. "Similarly the Holy One, blessed be He, said to all the mountains: "Since you wept over my sons when they

were exiled from their land....I shall bring the rejoicing of my sons
to the mountains...."
Pirqe Mashiah, BhM 3.73-74

In the above rabbinical text, notice that the Messiah is crowned in conjunction with the resurrection. Also there is an order to the resurrection. In the passage Ephraim (Messiah ben Joseph), the slain Messiah is alive once again, followed by the resurrection of Adam, then Abraham, Isaac, Jacob, and Moses, each in their respective order. Lastly, the second Adam is seen in between the lines of this passage, as the descendant of Adam, the Messiah, triumphs to restore man. The last paragraph of the above text is called an aggadah or story. It is interesting that the events associated with the resurrection are related to a wedding. Notice how all of this parallels the writing of Rav Shaul (Paul) to the Corinthian believers.

But now is Messiah risen from the dead, and become the firstfruits of them that slept. For since by man came death, by man came also the resurrection of the dead. For as in Adam all die, even so in Messiah shall all be made alive. But every man in his own order: Messiah the firstfruits; afterward they that are Messiah's at his coming....And so it is written, The first man Adam was made a living soul: the last Adam was made a quickening spirit. Howbeit that was not first which is spiritual, but that which is natural: and afterward that which is spiritual. The first man is of the earth, earthy: the second man is the lord from heaven. As is the earthy, such are they also that are earthy: and as is the heavenly, such are they also that are heavenly. And as we have borne the image of the earthy, we shall also bear the image of the heavenly.
I Corinthians 15.20-23,45-49

According to the Talmud, Rosh haShannah 16b, the resurrection of the dead will occur on Yom haDin (the Day of Judgment), which is also Rosh haShannah. From very ancient times, the resurrection of the dead has been associated with Rosh haShanah. Archaeologists are discovering Jewish tombstones with shofarim etched upon them, indicating their belief in a resurrection of the dead with the blowing of the shofar.

> And in the poetic conception of our later teachers, it was the sound of the great shofar that will on the Last Day rend open the graves, and cause the dead to rise. Thus, the Messianic Hope, Resurrection, and Immortality of the Soul are intertwined with the message of the Shofar.
> Hertz Authorized Daily Prayer Book, pg. 865

By the time of Yeshua, the subject of resurrection had become one of the most controversial topics, as evidenced in the gospels and the book of Acts. The Pharisees vehemently believed in the resurrection, while the Sadducees did not. The general public followed the teaching of the Pharisees in expectation of a resurrection of the righteous at the beginning of the Last Day (Messianic Kingdom.)

> Martha saith unto Him, I know that he shall rise again in the resurrection at the last day. Yeshua said to her, I am the Resurrection, and the Life: He that believeth in Me, though he were dead, yet shall he live. And whosoever liveth and believeth in Me shall never die. Believest thou this? She saith unto Him, Yea, L-rd: I believe that Thou art the Messiah, the Son of G-d, which should come into the world.
> Yochanan (John) 11.24-27

Earlier it was stated that Saadia Gaon, 9th century Jewish scholar, wrote ten reasons for the shofar to be blown on Rosh haShanah. The tenth reason has to do with the resurrection of the dead.

> The tenth reason is to remind us of the revival of the dead, that we may believe in it, as it is said (Isaiah 18.3): "All ye inhabitants of the world, and ye dwellers in the earth, when an ensign

(banner--symbolic of the Messiah) is lifted up on the mountains,
see ye; and when the horn is blown, hear ye."
Avudraham

According to Theodore Gaster and other Jewish scholars,[1]
the day of Rosh haShanah involves the sounding of the Last
Trump. Today one removed from understanding of such concepts
from Judaism as the Last Trump tends to give his and everybody
else's guess as to what these terms might mean. In order to
understand the passages in the gospels, epistles, and Revelation,
we must place these books back into their original Jewish context,
defining each term, phrase, and idiom the way the original writer
in his Jewish mode of thinking expressed it. Note the use of the
term "Last Trumpet" in I Corinthians fifteen in connection with
the resurrection of the dead.

> Now this I say, brethren, that flesh and blood cannot inherit the
> kingdom of G-d; neither doth corruption inherit incorruption.
> Behold, I show you a mystery, we shall not all sleep, but we shall
> all be changed, in a moment, in the twinkling of an eye, at the
> last trump: for the trumpet shall sound, and the dead shall be
> raised incorruptible, and we shall be changed. For this
> corruptible must put on incorruption, and this mortal must put
> on immortality. So when this corruptible shall have put on
> incorruption, and this mortal shall have put on immortality, then
> shall be brought to pass the saying that is written, Death is
> swallowed up in victory. O Death, where is thy sting? O Grave,
> where is thy victory? The sting of death is sin; and the strength
> of sin is the law. But thanks be to G-d, which giveth us the victory
> through our L-rd Yeshua Ha Mashiach.
> I Corinthians 15.50-55

Therefore, it should be realized that the ancient Jewish
understanding of the resurrection of the dead would occur at a
time known as the Last Trump and that this day is none other than

---

1) Kieval, Herman, The High Holy Days, (New York: The Burning Bush Press., 1959) pg.
    120

Rosh haShanah, the Day of the Sounding of the Trumpet, the announcement of the Messianic Kingdom.

From where, specifically, does the phrase "last trump" come? In Judaism there are three recognized shofarim or ram's horn trumpets. They are the first trump, the last trump, and the great shofar. These shofarim should not be confused with the two silver trumpets called chatzotzerah in Numbers 10. The first trump and the last trump relate to the two horns of a particular ram -- according to Jewish tradition the ram caught in the thicket on Mount Moriah when Abraham was ready to slay Isaac and offer him up as a burnt offering.[2] This ram became the substitute for Isaac, even as Yeshua the Messiah became the substitute for us and provided life for us through his death. In Pirke deR' Eliezer, a Rabbinic work, the left horn (first trump) was blown on Mt. Sinai[3] and its right horn (the last trump) will be blown to herald the coming of Messiah. An interesting question was posed by Rabbi Bechaye, "Was that ram not burnt, together with its horns, skin, and flesh? How could this be the source of the shofar that was blown on Mt. Sinai? The answer is that G-d created (resurrected) a new ram out of the ashes." The Great Shofar, as explained earlier, is the shofar blown at the conclusion of Yom Kippur, teaching of the ingathering of the exiles at the Messiah's literal second coming. Note that there is a difference between the last trump of Rosh haShanah, where the dead are resurrected and the believers are caught away, and that of the great shofar of Yom Kippur, where those who have become believers during the birthpangs are gathered from the four corners of the earth.

This passage from I Corinthians not only establishes the resurrection of the dead at Rosh haShannah, but it also states that

---

2)   Gen. 22.13

3)   Exo. 19.13

the living believers (Tzaddikim) will be caught away with them. Rav Shaul (the apostle Paul) wrote the same thing to the believers who were at Thessalonica.

> But I would not have you to be ignorant, brethren, concerning them which are asleep, that ye sorrow not, even as others which have no hope. For if we believe that Yeshua died and rose again, even so them also which sleep in Yeshua will G-d bring with Him. For this we say unto you by the word of the L-rd, that we which are alive and remain until the coming of the L-rd shall not prevent them which are asleep. For the L-rd Himself shall descend from heaven with a shout, with the voice of the archangel, and with the trumpet of G-d: and the dead in Messiah will rise first: then we which are alive and remain shall be caught up together with them in the clouds, to meet the L-rd in the air: and so shall we ever be with the L-rd. Wherefore comfort one another with these words.
>
> I Thessalonians 4.13-18

The reader should recall that on Yom haDin all the living are judged by G-d and divided into three separate groups: the tzaddikim (righteous), intermediate or average, and the rashim (wicked). The tzaddikim are separated and gathered to G-d for the coronation and wedding of His son, the Messiah, while the average and rashim enter into the Yamin Nora'im (Days of Awe) or the time of trouble.

Christian doctrines concerning the catching away of these believers in the Messiah have become some of the most controversial topics of discussion. The controversy, in one aspect, concerns the word "rapture," which is not a Biblical word, strictly speaking. Rav Shaul (Apostle Paul), in his letter to the Thessalonians, speaks of the resurrection of the dead at the blowing of the shofar, and of the tzaddikim who are alive being caught away. The Greek word for being "caught away" is harpuzo. This word, when translated into Latin, is the word raptiere. When

The Natzal and Ressurection   133

raptiere was translated into English and thus anglicized, the word rapture was coined. In this sense, the word is biblically based.

In Hebrew, three different terms are used for the dead and living tzaddikim in this resurrection and catching away. First is the word asaph, which means "to gather." When the shofar sounds at that six thousandth Rosh haShannah, the righteous will be gathered to the Messiah for his coronation.

> I saw in the night visions, and, behold, one like the son of man came with the clouds of heaven {the righteous}, and came to the Ancient of days, and they brought him near before him. And there was given him dominion, and glory, and a kingdom, that all people, nations, and languages, should serve him: his dominion is an everlasting dominion, which shall not pass away, and his kingdom that which shall not be destroyed.
> Daniel 7.13-14

A derivative of asaph is the word ne'esaph, a word that was used when a righteous man died and was gathered to his fathers. A note from the Gesenius Hebrew Lexicon on the word ne'esaph is interesting.

> NE'ESAPH - to be gathered to one's people, to one's father; used of entering into Hades, where the Hebrews regarded their ancestors as being gathered together. This gathering to one's fathers, or one's people, is distinguished both from death and burial.

> Then Abraham gave up the ghost, and died in a good old age, an old man, and full of years; and was gathered to his people.
> Genesis 25.8

> Behold therefore, I will gather thee unto thy fathers, and thou shalt be gathered into thy grave in peace; and thine eyes shall not see all the evil which I will bring upon this place. And they brought the king word again.
> II Kings 22.20

As explained above, those who are gathered are viewed as being alive even though their physical bodies are dead. These are those who are spoken of in I Thessalonians 4.14.

> For if we believe that Yeshua died and rose again, even so them also which sleep in Yeshua will G-d bring with him.
> I Thessalonians 4.14

Along with this ne'esaph, or gathering of the dead tzaddikim, will be the gathering of the living righteous.

> Gather yourselves together, yea, gather together, O nation not desired; before the decree bring forth, before the day pass as the chaff, before the fierce anger of the L-rd come upon you, before the day of the L-rd's anger come upon you. Seek ye the L-rd, all ye meek of the earth, which have wrought his judgment; seek righteousness, seek meekness: it may be ye shall be hid in the day of the L-rd's anger.
> Zephaniah 2.1-3

The Hebrew word for gathering that is used in the above passage is kashash -- a synonym for the word asaph, which denotes a collection. This gathering of both the living and dead tzaddikim will occur at the beginning of the Day of the L-rd as stated in II Thessalonians.

> Now we beseech you, brethren, by the coming of our L-rd Yeshua haMashiach, and by our gathering together unto him. That ye be not soon shaken in mind, or be troubled, neither by spirit, nor by word, nor by letter as from us, as that the day of Messiah is at hand. Let no man deceive you by any means: for that day shall not come, except there come a falling away first, and that man of sin be revealed, the son of perdition.
> II Thessalonians 2.1-3

Kenneth Wuest, a noted Greek scholar, states in his word studies an interesting point that has much to do with the catching away of the living believers. He states that the phrase "falling away" is a mistranslation of the Greek word apostasia and should rather be translated departure. "The root verb aphistemi is found fifteen times in the New Testament. It is translated 'depart' eleven times." Although it is often found translated in similar meanings, "the predominant meaning of this verb in the New Testament... is that of the act of a person departing from another person or from a place. . . Liddell and Scott in their classical lexicon give as the second meaning of apostasia, 'a departure, a disappearance.' Dr. E. Schuyler English, to whom the author is deeply indebted for calling his attention to the word 'departure' as the correct rendering of apostasia in this context, is authority for the fact that... the Greek word (means) 'a departure.'" Wuest further states that apostasia was at times used to denote a defection or revolt; however, this meaning "should not be imposed upon the word where the context does not qualify the word by these meanings."

According to Wuest, Rav Shaul (Apostle Paul) refers "to the gathering together of the saints, to the L-rd Yeshua at His coming, which is the departure of the congregation from the earth" in II Thessalonians 2.1. In Rav Shaul's previous letter, "he had described that event in the words, 'Then we which are alive and remain shall be caught up together with them in the clouds to meet the L-rd in the air,' which involves a departure from the earth."

Remember that the Greek word, harpuzo, means to catch away. Harpuzo is the word used in Rav Shaul's (Apostle Paul) first letter to the Thessalonians. Its Hebrew equivalent is natzal, which in its root form means to deliver. A derivative of natzal is metzal, which means to pluck away, or a radical departure.

Also the Greek word that is used in II Thessalonians 2.1 for this gathering is episunagoge, which is the Greek equivalent for asupah. Asupah is a derivative of the word asaph and is a word meaning the congregation, or assembly. According to Numbers 10.1-3, the assembly is gathered together by the blowing of the trumpet. Therefore, those that have received the Messiah and have been made as nobles are gathered to the gate of the assembly by the blowing of the trumpet.

> And the L-rd spake unto Moses, saying, make thee two trumpets of silver; of a whole piece shalt thou make them: that thou mayest use them for the calling of the assembly, and for the journeying of the camps. And when they shall blow with them, all the assembly shall assemble themselves to thee at the door of the tabernacle of the congregation.
> Numbers 10.1-3

As the believers are taken from the earth with the blowing of the shofar, they are in effect hidden from the wrath of G-d to come during the birthpains. The Talmudic name of Yom HaKeseh for this festival portrays this aspect.[4] The name means The Day of Concealment. It received this name from being the only festival that falls at the beginning of the month when the new moon may still be concealed. Remember that the Jewish calendar is a lunar calendar, and each new month will begin as the moon renews its thirty day cycle. G-d had prescribed that each New Moon, called Rosh Chodesh, was to be a special festival. According to Colossians 2.16-17, the New Moon was given to teach on the things to come, and the substance of the festival would be about the Messiah. In Genesis 1 the sun and the moon were given to be signs in the sky. Even though believers in the Messiah are not worshippers of the sun, it is recognized as being a picture of the Messiah.

> But unto you that fear my name shall the Sun of righteousness

---

4)   Beitzah 16a

The Natzal and Ressurection   137

(Messiah) arise with healing in his wings; and ye shall go forth, and grow up as calves of the stall.

Malachi 4.2

Likewise the moon is a picture of the believer. Because the moon goes through a cycle each month and therefore is renewed at the beginning of that cycle, it was said that it was being born again. During the new moon phase, the moon only reflects the smallest portion of the sun's light. Each day as the moon turns toward the sun, it reflects more and more of the sun. So it is with the believer, as he turns more toward the Messiah, he shows more of the Messiah in his own life.

Because the moon can hardly be seen at the New Moon, it is said to be hidden. For this reason, Psalm 81.3 was thought to speak of Rosh haShannah.

Blow the Shofar at the new moon, at the time of the concealed moon.

Psalm 81.3

Naturally, this is a picture of the believers' (the moon) being concealed at the time of the festival.

Therefore, when the earth reaches its six thousandth Rosh haShanah, the shofar will blow, calling to a resurrected life those that have believed in the Messiah. Those believers that are alive will be gathered together with them. The purpose of that gathering is to be present at the Messiah's coronation. In conjunction with the Messiah's coronation will be His wedding. Those that have believed in the Messiah from the time of Adam to the present are that bride, both Jew and Gentile. The fact that the believers are hidden from the wrath on the earth is a by-product of the gathering, rather than its main objective.

CHAPTER 11

THE CORONATION

One of the concepts in Jewish liturgy and tradition for Rosh haShanah is "Ha Melech," which means "The King." Rosh haShanah's essential message is the reaffirmation of the kingship of G-d. For this reason, it is known as the "day of the coronation."[1] In the service for Rosh haShanah, there are special readings such as the portion Malkuyot, and songs such as "Avinu Malkenu," (Our Father, Our King) expressing this idea.

Looking at the Scriptures concerning Rosh haShanah, it becomes obvious that it is the coronation of the Messiah. From ancient times, Jewish scholars have always associated this Day with the beginning of the Messianic Kingdom, hence a Messianic King.

Prophecies concerning a coming king are very ancient. Observe these:

> The sceptre shall not depart from Judah, nor a lawgiver from between his feet until Shiloh (a name for the Messiah) come; and unto him shall the gathering of the people be.
> Genesis 49.10

> I shall see him, but not now: I shall behold him, but not nigh: there shall come a Star out of Jacob, and a Sceptre shall arise out of Israel, and shall smite the corners of Moab, and destroy all the children of Sheth.
> Numbers 24.17

---

1) Kieval, Herman, The High Holy Days, (New York: The Burning Bush Press, 1959), pg. 42-43

The ruler mentioned above is to come from the tribe of Judah. This prophecy was realized by King David. However, G-d made a promise concerning a particular descendant of David.

> Behold, the days come, saith the L-rd, that I will raise unto David a righteous Branch, and a King shall reign and prosper, and shall execute judgment and justice in the earth.
> Jeremiah 23.5

Yeshua is the fulfillment of this prophecy. Indeed, at his conception it was announced by an angel from G-d:

> He shall be great, and shall be called the Son of the Highest: and the L-rd G-d shall give unto him the throne of his father David: and He shall reign over the house of Jacob forever; and of his kingdom there shall be no end.
> Luke 1.32,33

Was Yeshua ever recognized as king? He was referred to during his lifetime as the Son of David, the King of the Jews, and the King of Israel. Both His lineage and His fulfillment of Messianic prophecies caused people to recognize Him as King.

> Nathanael saith unto him, whence knowest thou me? Yeshua answered and said unto him, before that Philip called thee, when thou wast under the fig tree, I saw thee. Nathanael answered, and saith unto him, Rabbi, thou art the Son of G-d; thou art the King of Israel
> Yochanan (John) 1.48-49

When Yeshua came into Jerusalem for the last time, He was riding on a donkey. The crowd recognized his credentials from all He had said and done, hailing Him as their King.

> Rejoice greatly, O daughter of Zion; shout O daughter of Jerusalem: behold thy king cometh unto thee: He is just and having salvation, lowly and riding upon an ass, and upon a colt, the foal of an ass.
> Zechariah 9.9

And when He was come nigh, even now at the descent of the Mt. of Olives, the whole multitude of the disciples began to rejoice and praise G- d with a loud voice for all the mighty works that they had seen; saying, Blessed be the King that cometh in the name of the L-rd: Peace in heaven, and glory in the highest.
Luke 19.37,38

In order to have a king, there must be a coronation. The Messiah Yeshua will have a literal crowning in the future at a Rosh haShanah. In the following passage, there are two phrases which identify the scene as Rosh haShanah. Daniel 7.9-10 is obviously Yom haDin, the day of judgment, as the court is seated, and the books are opened. The Ancient of Days, G-d, is seated to judge all men.

I beheld till the thrones were cast down, and the Ancient of days did sit, whose garment was white as snow, and the hair of his head like the pure wool: his throne was like the fiery flame, and his wheels as burning fire. A fiery stream issued and came forth from before him: thousand thousands ministered unto him, and ten thousand times ten thousand stood before him: the judgment was set, and the books were opened.
Daniel 7:9-10

In verses 13 and 14, the Son of Man (a term for Messiah) comes to the Ancient of Days and is given a kingdom (coronation).

I saw in the night visions, and, behold, one like the Son of man came with the clouds of heaven, and came to the Ancient of days, and they brought him near before him. And there was given him dominion, and glory, and a kingdom, that all people, nations, and languages, should serve him: his dominion is an everlasting dominion, which shall not pass away, and his kingdom that which shall not be destroyed.
Daniel 7:13-14

A companion passage is found in Revelation, chapters four

and five. At the beginning of chapter four, there is the sounding of the Shofar, indicating Rosh haShanah. Again, it is the court of heaven with G-d the Father sitting on the throne till chapter five, when the Messiah is given the Kingdom. Notice that the coronation takes place and that Yochanan (writer of Revelation), actually was summoned by the trumpet to witness this event.

After this I looked, and, behold, a door was opened in heaven. And the first voice which I heard was as it were of a trumpet talking with me; which said, come up hither, and I will show thee things which must be hereafter. And immediately I was in the Spirit: and, behold, a throne was set in heaven, and one sat on the throne. And he that sat was to look upon like a jasper and a sardine stone: and there was a rainbow round about the throne, in sight like unto an emerald. And round about the throne were four and twenty seats: and upon the seats I saw four and twenty elders sitting, clothed in white raiment; and they had on their heads crowns of gold. And out of the throne proceeded lightnings, and thunderings, and voices: and there were seven lamps of fire burning before the throne, which are the seven Spirits of G-d. And before the throne there was a sea of glass like unto crystal. And in the midst of the throne, and round about the throne, were four beasts full of eyes before and behind. And the first beast was like a lion, and the second beast like a calf, and the third beast had a face as a man, and the fourth beast was like a flying eagle. And the four beasts had each of them six wings about him; and they were full of eyes within: and they rest not day and night, saying, Holy, holy, holy, L-rd G-d Almighty, which was, and is, and is to come.

Revelation 4.1-8

And when those beasts give glory and honour and thanks to him that sat on the throne, who liveth for ever and ever, the four and twenty elders fall down before him that sat on the throne, and worship him that liveth forever and ever, and cast their crowns before the throne, saying, Thou art worthy, O L-rd, to receive glory and honour and power: for thou hast created all things, and for thy pleasure they are and were created. And I saw in the right hand of him that sat on the throne a book written within and

The Coronation

on the backside sealed with seven seals. and I saw a strong angel proclaiming with a loud voice, Who is worthy to open the book, and to loose the seals thereof? And no man in heaven, nor in earth, neither under the earth, was able to open the book, neither to look thereon. And I wept much, because no man was found worthy to open and to read the book, neither to look thereon. And one of the elders saith unto me, Weep not: behold, the Lion of the tribe of Judah, the Root of David, hath prevailed to open the book, and to loose the seven seals thereof. And I beheld, and, lo, in the midst of the throne and of the four beasts, and in the midst of the elders, stood a Lamb as it had been slain, having seven horns and seven eyes, which are the seven Spirits of G-d sent forth into all the earth. And he came and took the book out of the right hand of him that sat upon the throne. And when he had taken the book, the four beasts and four and twenty elders fell down before the Lamb, having every one of them harps, and golden vials full of odours, which are the prayers of saints. And they sung a new song, saying, Thou art worthy to take the book, and to open the seals thereof: for thou wast slain, and hast redeemed us to G- d by thy blood out of every kindred, and tongue, and people, and nation; and hast made us unto our G-d kings and priests: and we shall reign on the earth. And I beheld, and I heard the voice of many angels round about the throne, and the beasts, and the elders: and the number of them was ten thousand times ten thousand, and thousands of thousands; saying with a loud voice, Worthy is the Lamb that was slain to receive power, and riches, and wisdom, and strength, and honor, and glory, and blessing. And every creature which is in heaven, and on the earth, and under the earth, and such as are in the sea, and all that are in them, heard I saying, Blessing, and honour, and glory and power be unto Him that sitteth upon the throne, and unto the Lamb for ever and ever. And the four beasts said, Amen. And the four and twenty elders fell down and worshipped Him that liveth for ever and ever.
Revelation 4.9-5.14

Many of the Psalms speak of the coronation of the Messiah such as Psalms two and forty-seven.

Why do the heathen rage, and the people imagine a vain thing?

The Coronation 143

The kings of the earth set themselves, and the rulers take counsel together, against the L-rd, and against His Anointed (Messiah), saying, Let us break Their bands asunder, and cast away Their cords from us. He that sitteth in the heavens shall laugh: the L-rd shall have them in derision. Then shall He speak unto them in His wrath, and vex them in His sore displeasure. Yet have I set my King upon my holy hill of Zion. I will declare the decree: The L-rd hath said unto Me, Thou art My Son; this day have I begotten Thee. Ask of Me, and I shall give Thee the heathen for Thine inheritance, and the uttermost parts of the earth for Thy possession. Thou shalt break them with a rod of iron; Thou shalt dash them in pieces like a potter's vessel. Be wise now therefore, O ye kings: be instructed, ye judges of the earth. Serve the L-rd with fear, and rejoice with trembling. Kiss the Son, lest He be angry, and ye perish from the way, when His wrath is kindled but a little. Blessed are all they that put their trust in Him.

Psalm two

In Judaism, Psalm 2.12 is a very controversial verse. This verse is translated differently in Bibles, depending on whether the publisher is a Jewish or non- Jewish enterprise. Below is the verse as is written in the Harkavy Edition of the Holy Scripture:

Arm yourselves with purity, lest He be angry, and ye perish from the way, when His wrath is kindled but a little. Blessed are all they that put their trust in Him.

Psalm 2.12 Harkavy

The same verse, however, appears in the King James translation as follows:

Kiss the Son, lest He be angry, and ye perish from the way, when His wrath is kindled but a little. Blessed are all they that put their trust in Him.

Psalm 2.12 King James

It is established from the Midrashim, however, that the verse as it is written in most Gentile published Bibles does not contradict the ancient understanding.

In another comment the verse is read, "Do homage to the son," (Psalm 2.12). What parable fits here? That of a king who became angry at the inhabitants of a certain city, and the inhabitants of the city went and pleaded with the king's son to mollify the king. So he went and mollified his father. After the king was mollified by his son, the inhabitants of the city were about to sing a song of homage to the king. But the king said to them:

"Is it to me that ye would sing a song of homage? Go and sing the song of homage to my son: had it not been for him, I would long ago have destroyed the inhabitants of this city." Likewise, when the peoples of the earth will be told "O clap your hands, all ye peoples; shout unto G-d with the voice of triumph," (Psalm 47.2) and will be about to sing a song of homage to the Holy One, blessed be He, the Holy One, blessed be He, will say: "Is it to Me that ye would sing a song of homage? Go and sing it to Israel. Had it not been for them, the earth would not have endured for a single hour, for it is said, "If I whet My glittering sword, and My hand take hold on judgment . . . I will make Mine arrows drunk with blood . . . Sing aloud, O ye nations, to His people," (Deuteronomy 32.41-43)."
The Midrash on Psalms

Psalm forty-seven is a recurring passage throughout the Rosh haShanah liturgy. Its emphasis on the coronation of the Messiah is obvious.

O clap your hands, all ye people, shout unto G-d with the voice of triumph. For the L-rd Most High is terrible; He is a great King over all the earth. He shall subdue the people under us, and the nations under our feet. He shall choose our inheritance for us, the excellency of Jacob whom He loved. Selah. G-d is gone up with a shout, the L-rd with the sound of a trumpet. Sing praises to G-d, sing praises: sing praises unto our King, sing praises. For G-d is the King of all the earth: sing ye praises with understanding. G-d reigneth over the heathen: G-d sitteth upon the throne of His holiness. The princes of the people are

gathered together, even the people of the G-d of Abraham: for the shields of the earth belong unto G-d: He is greatly exalted.
Psalm Forty-seven

CHAPTER 12

THE WEDDING OF THE MESSIAH

In order to understand the next aspect of Rosh haShanah, one must be familiar with some of the ancient Jewish wedding customs. An amazing picture evolves when these customs are placed side by side with the festivals. For the young man of Israel, to be married, bear children, and assume his responsibilities in the Jewish community were the prime goals of his life. From the time of his Bar Mitzvah at age thirteen until about age twenty is the time in which he would be expected to take a wife. In ancient Israel there was no dating, nor was there a group known as teenagers. One went from childhood to adulthood; there was no adolescence period.

Many marriages were arranged by parents from the time that their children were infants. Others, however, went through the following process: At marrying age, the young man might be attracted to a young woman, or his parents might have chosen an appropriate bride for him. The procedure could be followed by one of three different parties: the father making the arrangements for his son, as Samson's father did for him,[1] an agent working on behalf of the father, as Eliezer did on behalf of Abraham,[2] or the young man himself.[3] For illustration's sake, an example of the last possibility will be used.

---

1) Jud. 14.1-10

2) Gen. Twenty-four

3) Gen. 29.15-30

A young man went to the home of his potential bride-to-be. He carried three things with him: a large sum of money in order to pay the price for his bride, a betrothal contract called a Shitre Erusin, and a skin of wine. Of course, anyone arriving with these things would immediately be under suspicion. The man approached the girl's father and older brothers. The contract was laid out, and the bride-price was discussed. Finally, a glass of wine was poured. If the father approved, then the maiden was called in. If she also approved, then she would drink the wine. In doing so, she committed herself to this man, agreeing to follow the contract that now was a legal document between the two. They would be called husband and wife at this time, and their union could only be dissolved by a divorce.[4] However, their status was that of betrothed, rather than that of fully married.

After the wine had been drunk, the man made the statement that he would go to his father's house and prepare a place for her. This place is known as the chadar (chamber), sometimes referred to as the chupah (or honeymoon bed). From the time that the Shitre Erusin was ratified, the young woman was consecrated -- set apart to her husband.[5] She has been bought with a price.[6] She must spend her time preparing to live as a wife and mother in Israel. Her days of waiting for her wedding are spent in learning how to please her husband.

Meanwhile, the young man returned to his father's home, and the chadar goes under construction. The room is provided with every comfort, as they will retire here for one week following their

---

4) Foote-Moore, George, Judaism in the First Century Christian Era, Vol. II, (Cambridge: Harvard University Press, 1927) pg. 121

5) ibid: pg. 122

6) The bridal price or present is known as the Mohar. Gen 24.12; Ex. 22.17; I Sam. 18.25

wedding ceremony. The young man, if asked when the day of his wedding will be, replies, "No man knows except my father."[7] In Israel the father had to be satisfied that every preparation had been made by his son before he gave him permission to go and get his bride.

The groom designated two close friends to assist him in securing his bride and during the actual ceremony. These two are known as "the friends of the bridegroom."[8] They functioned as the two witnesses required for a Jewish wedding.[9] One of them was assigned to assist the bride, and to lead her to the ceremony, while the other was stationed with the groom.[10] He performed a special task when the couple retired into the chadar after the ceremony.

During the ceremony, known as Kedushin, a second contract was brought forth called a Ketubah. This marriage contract was witnessed by the friends of the bridegroom and turned over to the parents of the bride. It contained the promises that the groom

7)   Mk. 13.32

8)   Edersheim, Alfred, Sketches of Jewish Social Life, (Grand Rapids: Wm. B. Erdman's Publishing Company, 1982), pgs. 152-153

9)   ibid

10) ibid

The Wedding of the Messiah   **149**

pledged to his wife. The ceremony was very much like the Jewish wedding of today. As at all weddings, focus was centered on the bride and groom. For this one day they were looked at as king and queen.[11] Every effort was taken, and every possible expense was made to insure their joy. On this day, tradition says, their sins are forgiven.[12] They stand pure, without spot or blemish as they are united.

Following the ceremony, the bride and groom entered the chadar. Here the groom gave gifts to the bride.[13] The couple spent seven days under the chupah.[14] The friend of the bridegroom stood at the door. All the guests of the wedding assembled outside, waiting for the friend of the bridegroom to announce the consummation of the marriage, which was related to him by the groom.[15] At this signal, great rejoicing broke forth in a week-long celebration,[16] until the two emerged from the chupah to begin the actual wedding feast.[17]

Throughout the Scriptures, the terminology of the wedding is applied to the relationship between Messiah and his bride. The analogy can be seen in the spring festivals of a young man going through the betrothal ceremony. Even as the believers have

11) Taamey haMinhagim 961; Midrash Talpioth, s.v. Chathan VeKallah; Mataamim haChadash 46, from psa. 89.20.

12) Midrash Talpioth. s.v. Chathan VeKallah.

13) Gen. 34.12; 24.53

14) Kaplan, Rabbi Aryeh, Made in Heaven, (New York: Moznaim Publishing, 1979), pgs. 230-233.

15) Jn. 3.29; ibid pg. 208

16) ibid

17) Joel 2.16; Luke 12.35-37

The Wedding of the Messiah

become the betrothed wife of the Messiah,[18] we now await the wedding and all that follows as promised in the fall festivals.

Yeshua, at the Passover meal the night before He was slain, made the speech that a young Jewish bridegroom leaving to build the chadar would make.

> In my Father's house are many mansions: if it were not so, I would have told you. I go to prepare a place for you. And if I go and prepare a place for you, I will come again, and receive you unto myself; that where I am, there ye may be also.
> Yochanan (John) 14.2-3

The wine that was drunk that night is clearly associated with the sealing of the Shitre Erusin.[19] Rav Shaul (the Apostle Paul) said that the Messiah's death for our sins was the same as the young man's paying for his bride.

> For ye are bought with a price: therefore glorify G-d in your body, and in your spirit which are G-d's.
> I Corinthians 6.20

The body of believers as the bride, is called consecrated -- set apart, bought with a price.

> Ye are bought with a price: be not ye the servants of men.
> I Corinthians 7.23

We even see one of the friends of the bridegroom in Yochanan (John). He speaks of standing next to the door waiting for the consummation of the marriage.

> He that hath the bride is the bridegroom: but the friend of the bridegroom, which standeth and heareth him, rejoiceth greatly

---

18) Eph. 5.22-33

19) Lk. 22.17-18; Mk. 14.23-25; Mt. 26.27-29

The Wedding of the Messiah   **151**

> because of the bridegroom's voice: this my joy therefore is
> fulfilled.
>
> Yochanan (John) 3.29

The other friend of the bridegroom, the one assigned to the bride, is seen in Exodus nineteen, as Moses leads Israel, the bride of the Messiah, to meet her G-d at Mt. Sinai.[20] In fact, Shavuot is recorded as the betrothal between Israel and the L-rd.

> Go and cry in the ears of Jerusalem, saying, Thus saith the L-rd;
> I remember thee, the kindness of thy youth, the love of thine
> espousals (betrothal), when thou wentest after me in the
> wilderness, in a land that was not sown.
>
> Jeremiah 2.2-3

Even as the first trump (shofar) announced the betrothal, so will the last trump announce the wedding. In Psalm Forty-five we are brought to the Biblical portrayal of not only the wedding of the Messiah but also His coronation. The guests are assembled, and gifts are distributed.

> My heart is indicting a good matter: I speak of the things which
> I have made touching the King: my tongue is the pen of a ready
> writer. Thou art fairer than the children of men: grace is poured
> into thy lips: therefore G-d hath blessed thee for ever. Gird thy
> sword upon thy thigh. O most mighty, with thy glory and thy
> majesty. And in thy majesty ride prosperously, because of truth
> and meekness and righteousness; and thy right hand shall teach
> thee terrible things. Thine arrows are sharp in the heart of the
> King's enemies; whereby the people fall under thee. Thy throne,
> O G-d is, for ever and ever: the sceptre of thy kingdom is a right
> sceptre. Thou lovest righteousness, and hatest wickedness:
> therefore G-d, thy G-d, hath anointed thee with the oil of gladness
> above thy fellows. All thy garments smell of myrrh, and aloes,
> and cassia, out of the ivory palaces, whereby they have made
> thee glad. Kings' daughters were among thy honourable

---

20) Ex. 19.17

The Wedding of the Messiah

women: upon thy right hand did stand the queen in gold of Ophir. Hearken, O daughter, and consider, and incline thine ear; forget also thine own people, and thy father's house. So shall the King greatly desire thy beauty: for he is thy L-rd; and worship thou him. And the daughter of Tyre shall be there with a gift; even the rich among the people shall entreat thy favour. The King's daughter is all glorious within: her clothing is of wrought gold. She shall be brought unto the king in raiment of needlework: the virgins her companions that follow her shall be brought unto thee. With gladness and rejoicing shall they be brought: they shall enter into the King's palace. Instead of thy fathers' shall be thy children whom thou mayest make princes in all the earth. I will make thy name to be remembered in all generations: therefore shall the people praise thee for ever and ever.
Psalm Forty-five

The following passage shows the glory of the bride and groom bedecked in all their wedding finery:

I will greatly rejoice in the L-rd, my soul shall be joyful in my G-d; for He hath clothed me with the garments of salvation, He hath covered me with the robe of righteousness, as a bridegroom decketh himself with ornaments, and as a bride adorneth herself with her jewels. For as the earth bringeth forth her bud, and as the garden causeth the things that are sown in it to spring forth; so the L-rd G-d will cause righteousness and praise to spring forth before all the nations. For Zion's sake will I not hold My peace, and for Jerusalem's sake I will not rest, until the righteousness thereof go forth as brightness, and the salvation thereof as a lamp that burneth. And the Gentiles shall see Thy righteousness, and all kings Thy glory: and Thou shalt be called by a new name, which the mouth of the L-rd shall name. Thou shalt also be a crown of glory in the hand of the L-rd, and a royal diadem in the hand of thy G-d. Thou shalt no more be termed Forsaken; neither shall thy land any more be termed Desolate: but thou shalt be called Hephzibah,[21] and thy land Beulah:[22] for

21) Literal translation: "My delight is in her"

22) Literal translation: "Married"

the L-rd delighteth in thee, and thy land shall be married. For as a young man marrieth a virgin, so shall thy sons marry thee: and as the bridegroom rejoices over the bride, so shall thy G-d rejoice over thee.

Isaiah 61:10-62:5

Once the ceremony is completed, the two retire to the bridal chamber. Shir HaShirim, the Song of Songs, which is read during Pesach, gives details of the intimacy between the Messiah and His Love. The seven days of the chupah relate to the seven years between the Messiah's coronation and wedding, and his second coming to earth.

During this time the bride will be "remembered" by G-d, and given gifts.

Then they that feared the L-rd spake often one to another: and the L-rd hearkened, and heard it, and a book of remembrance was written before him for them that feared the L-rd, and that thought upon his name. And they shall be mine, saith the L-rd of hosts, in that day when I make up my jewels and I will spare them, as a man spareth his own son that serveth him.

Malachi 3.16,17

In Joel 2.15 we are brought back to the stark reality of what has been happening on earth. The time is Yom Kippur. The bride and bridegroom are coming out of the chupah. The believers on earth are crying out to G-d to come to their aid.[23] In Joel 2.23 we see again the Messiah's coming as illustrated by the latter and former rain. We are told that His comings will be in the first month. The first coming in which He died and was resurrected was in Aviv, the first month of the religious calendar; whereas, His second coming will be in Tishri, the first month of the civil calendar. As related in previous chapters, the Shofar haGadol is blown.

---

23) Joel 2.17-18

Joel 2.15 refers to Yom Kippur, established by the blowing of the shofar and the consecrating of the fast. This shofar would be the "Shofar haGadol," or "Great Shofar." See Mattatiyahu (Matthew) 24.31. This shofar is blown during the last ceremony of Yom Kippur known as "Neilah," the "closing of the gate."

> Blow the trumpet in Zion, sanctify a fast (Yom Kippur), call a solemn assembly. Gather the people, sanctify the congregation, assemble the elders, gather the children, and those that suck the breasts: let the bridegroom go forth of his chamber, and the bride out of her closet. Let the priests, the ministers of the L-rd, weep between the porch and the altar (which was done at Yom Kippur), and let them say, Spare thy people, O L-rd, and give not thine heritage to reproach, that the heathen should rule over them: wherefore should they say among the people, Where is their G-d? Be glad then, ye children of Zion, and rejoice in the L-rd your G-d: for he hath given you the former rain moderately, and he will cause to come down for you the rain, the former rain, and the latter rain in the first month.
>
> Joel 2.15-17,23

At this time the angels will go forth to gather the scattered believers to Jerusalem to participate in the next appointment there, Sukkot. A central theme of the feast of Sukkot is the wedding feast.[24]

> And I heard as it were the voice of a great multitude, and as the voice of many waters, and as the voice of mighty thunderings, saying, Alleluia: for the L-rd G-d omnipotent reigneth. Let us be glad and rejoice, and give honour to him: for the marriage of the Lamb is come, and his wife hath made herself ready. And to her was granted that she should be arrayed in fine linen, clean and white: for the fine linen is the righteousness of saints. And he saith unto me, Write, Blessed are they which are called unto the marriage supper of the Lamb. And he saith unto me, These are true sayings of G-d. And I saw heaven opened, and behold a

---

24) Gen. 29.23-28

The Wedding of the Messiah 155

white horse; and he that sat upon him was called Faithful and True, and in righteousness he doth judge and make war. And he hath on his vesture and on his thigh a name written, KING OF KINGS, AND L-RD OF L-RDS. And I saw an angel standing in the sun; and he cried with a loud voice, saying to all the fowls that fly in the midst of heaven, Come and gather yourselves together unto the supper of the great G-d: That ye may eat the flesh of kings, and the flesh of captains, and the flesh of mighty men, and the flesh of horses, and of them that sit on them, and the flesh of all men, both free and bond, both small and great.

Revelation 19.6-9,11,16-18

Let your loins be girded about, and your lights burning; and ye yourselves like unto men that wait for their lord, when he will return from the wedding; that, when he cometh and knocketh, they may open unto him immediately. Blessed are those servants, whom the lord when he cometh shall find watching: verily, I say unto you, that he shall gird himself, and make them to sit down to meat, and will come forth and serve them.

Luke 12.35-37

The Wedding of the Messiah

CHAPTER 13

EPILOGUE

The message of Rosh haShanah more than any time in the past should now be heard. Israel is an independent nation once again. Jerusalem, as prophesied, has returned to the Jewish people. We are close to the conclusion of 6,000 years since the garden of Eden, and the time for the shofar to blow is at hand.

Just as in the yearly Jewish calendar there is a season of Teshuvah, so can it be expected in the eschatological calendar. As the Messiah is expected to return on Yom Kippur, the last day of the season of Teshuvah, so should the last forty years be a picture of this season. Yeshua, in the parable of the fig tree, alluded to this last forty-year period.

> And He spake to them a parable; Behold the fig tree, and all the tree; When they now shoot forth, ye see and know of your own selves that summer is now nigh at hand. So likewise ye, when ye see these things come to pass, know ye that the kingdom of G-d is nigh at hand. Verily I say unto you, This generation shall not pass away, till all be fulfilled. Heaven and earth shall pass away: but My words shall not pass away.
> Luke 21.29-33

These words, spoken by Yeshua haMashiach shortly before His death on the tree, were to answer three questions the disciples had asked Him regarding His second coming:

> And as He sat upon the mount of Olives, the disciples came unto Him privately, saying, Tell us, when shall these things be? and what shall be the sign of thy coming, and of the end of the world?
> Mattatiyahu 24.3

Note that He instructed us to observe the Fig Tree and that when we see her begin to blossom, it would be time for His return. Who is this Fig Tree according to the Scriptures, and what is meant by her beginning to blossom or to bud?

As to the identity of the Fig Tree, the ancient Hebrew prophets leave no doubt:

> I found Israel like grapes in the wilderness; I saw your fathers as the firstripe in the fig tree at her first time.
> Hosea 9.10

Also, the prophet Joel, speaking of the Assyrian invasion of Israel, said this:

> For a nation is come up upon my land, strong, and without number, whose teeth are the teeth of a lion, and he hath the cheek teeth of a great lion. He hath laid my vine waste, and barked my fig tree: he hath made it clean bare, and cast it away; the branches thereof are made white.
> Joel 1.6-7

So we see that in the parable of Luke Twenty-one, the Fig Tree is Israel. Many people have felt that Israel's becoming a nation again in 1948, after a 2,000- year dispersion, was the fulfillment of this prophecy; but let's return to Scripture and see if the blossoming is defined by G-d.

For 1,500 years, the Jewish prophets and the Scriptures had spoken of the Coming One. The whole nation of Israel was awaiting this man, the Messiah. Unfortunately, although many thousands of Jews received Yeshua as their Messiah, as a nation, Israel did not. Because she did not know Him when He came, Yeshua foretold her destruction:

> And when He was come near, He beheld the city, and wept over it, Saying, If thou hadst known, even thou, at least in this thy day, the things which belong unto thy peace! but now they are hid

Epilogue

from thine eyes. For the days shall come upon thee, that thine enemies shall cast a trench about thee, and compass thee round, and keep thee in on every side, And shall lay thee even with the ground, and thy children within thee; and they shall not leave in thee one stone upon another; because thou knewest not the time of thy visitation.

Luke 19.41-44

This brings understanding to another passage on the Fig Tree:

Now in the morning as He returned into the city, He hungered. And when He saw a fig tree in the way, He came to it, and found nothing thereon, but leaves only, and said unto it, Let no fruit grow on thee henceforward for ever. And presently the fig tree withered away.

Mattatiyahu (Matthew) 21.18-19

True to both prophecies of the destruction of Israel, forty years later the Roman army of Titus destroyed Jerusalem and dispersed Israel. For 2,000 years the Jewish people wandered from nation to nation without a homeland as prophesied by Hosea 6.1-3 and Jeremiah 50.4-8, until 1948 when Israel became a nation once again. As already stated, many people regard this as the fulfillment of the blossoming of Israel.

Is it? The Fig Tree was cursed for not having fruit on it. What was the expected fruit? It was for Israel to receive Yeshua as their Messiah. Therefore, since Israel in 1948 was no closer to having received her Messiah than in 30 C.E., how could this be a fulfillment of Luke Twenty-one?

However, Rav Shaul (the Apostle Paul) tells us in the book of Romans that there will be a time when Israel will accept the Messiah:

For I would not, brethren, that ye should be ignorant of this mystery, lest ye should be wise in your own conceits; that

Epilogue

> blindness in part is happened to Israel, until the fullness of the Gentiles be come in. And so all Israel shall be saved: as it is written, There shall come out of Zion the Deliverer, and shall turn away ungodliness from Jacob: For this is my covenant unto them, when I shall take away their sins.
>
> Romans 11.25-27

According to this prophecy, when the time of the Gentiles is fulfilled, Jews should begin to accept Yeshua as the Messiah in large numbers. Yeshua said concerning Israel and Jerusalem:

> And they shall fall by the edge of the sword, and shall be led away captive into all nations: and Jerusalem shall be trodden down of the Gentiles, until the times of the Gentiles be fulfilled.
>
> Luke 21.24

On May 14, 1948, even as Israel declared its independence, the Arab states surrounding this tiny, new nation began a war of annihilation. To their amazement, as well as the world's, the impossible began to happen, for Israel began to capture territory rather than lose it. Israel, having less than one million, was fighting equipped armies of several nations representing 82 million Arabs, and was emerging as the victor. If Jerusalem had fallen into Israeli hands at this time, then according to Scripture, the times of the Gentiles would have been fulfilled; and spiritual blindness would have begun to fall away from Israel. In the midst of the battle for Jerusalem, as the Israeli troops were sweeping through the city, confident of its capture, an amazing thing happened -- the United Nations called for a cease-fire. Why? Simply, it was not the timing of G-d.

On June 7, 1967, (around Shavuoth or Pentecost) during the Six Day War, Israel recaptured Jerusalem from Arab Jordan. True to the prophecy, blindness is falling off Israel and they are receiving Yeshua as their Messiah. It is believed that more Jews have received Yeshua since 1967 than in the 1,900 years since the first century.

Yes, today we are seeing the blossoming of the Fig Tree and all the trees, as G-d is pouring out His Spirit on all flesh. The focal point of this pouring out of the Spirit is Israel and the Jewish people.

Stopping to reflect on this for a moment, one will realize that this was the time when G-d began the outpouring of the Spirit that eventually spread around the world.

> And when the day of Pentecost was fully come, they were all with one accord in one place. And suddenly there came a sound from heaven as of a rushing mighty wind, and it filled all the house where they were sitting. And there appeared unto them cloven tongues like as of fire, and it sat upon each of them. And they were all filled with the Ruach haKodesh (the Holy Spirit), and began to speak with other tongues, as the Spirit gave them utterance.
>
> Acts 2.1-4

This Shavuot was the beginning of the Messianic Jewish movement. In the days following, literally thousands of Jewish men, women, and children gave their lives to the Messiah.

> Then they that gladly received his word were immersed: and the same day there were added unto them about three thousand souls. And they continued steadfastly in the apostles' doctrine and fellowship, and in breaking of bread, and in prayers. And they, continuing daily with one accord in the temple, and breaking bread from house to house, did eat their meat with gladness and singleness of heart, Praising G-d, and having favour with all the people. And the L-rd added to the congregation daily such as should be saved.
>
> Acts 2.41,42,46,47

As one reads the book of Acts, it becomes obvious that the Jewish believers in Yeshua remained Jewish. They worshipped in the Temple, attended synagogues, observed the Sabbath, and all of the Jewish Feasts. In fact, Jacob (James), the brother of Yeshua, made this statement to Rav Shaul (Paul):

> And when they heard it, they glorified the L-rd, and said unto him, Thou seest, brother, how many thousands of Jews there are which believe; and they are all zealous of the Torah (law).
> Acts 21.20

All of these customs, traditions, and observances were not done for their salvation, but rather in the fullness of the Messiah of whom these things were about.

Even so, today, in the modern Messianic movement, Jewish believers are remaining culturally Jews. Throughout the United States, in practically every major city, as well as many smaller ones, Messianic synagogues are being established. Here, both Jewish and Gentile believers praise Yeshua in a Davidic worship, reminiscent of the first century, complete with Shabbat (Sabbath), festivals, song and dance; and all of these center in Yeshua.

Possibly as many as 100,000 Jews in the United States have received Yeshua as the Messiah since 1967. Not only here, but throughout the world, G-d is moving among the Jewish people for salvation and giving them a Messianic vision to remain as a Jew. Today, there are Messianic congregations in England, France, several other European countries, Ethiopia, Mexico, Australia, and even Turkey .

> Thus saith the L-rd of hosts; In those days it shall come to pass, that ten men shall take hold out of all languages of the nations, even shall take hold of the skirt of him that is a Jew, saying, We will go with you: for we have heard that G-d is with you.
> Zechariah 8.23

This outpouring of G-d's Spirit upon the Jewish people will in turn affect the entire world.

> Verily I say unto you, This generation shall not pass away, till all be fulfilled. Heaven and earth shall pass away: but My words shall not pass away.
>
> Luke 21.32-33

With the blowing of the shofar, the graves will be opened, and the dead in Messiah with the remnant who are alive will be caught up with him in the air to experience his coronation and to join hand-in-hand with him in the Kedushin, the wedding ceremony. The rewards will be given, and the seven days of the chupah will occur. On earth the shofar blast will bring days of horror that no man can fully comprehend at present. The false messiah will arise in the world. He will make war on those who turn to G-d during this time of trouble. At the end of the seven years, as the Messiah and His bride emerge from the chupah, He will hear their cry and will come forth as the conquering King. The Great Shofar will be blown, and the believers will all be gathered to Jerusalem to experience Messiah's victory. A great banquet will be spread, and a new era is enjoyed by those present.

A final note - an ancient Temple prayer with a theme that has passed down from generation to generation is a cry to all mankind as the day of Rosh haShanah approaches, yearly and prophetically. It is recorded for us by Rav Shaul (the apostle Paul) in Ephesians 5.14:

> Wherefore he saith, Awake thou that sleepest, and arise from the dead, and Messiah shall give thee light. See then that ye walk circumspectly, not as fools but as wise, redeeming the time, because the days are evil. Wherefore be ye not unwise, but understanding what the will of the L-rd is.
>
> Ephesians 5.14-17

Epilogue

Epilogue

BIRTH OF YESHUA DURING SUKKOT

An easy to document, but not well known fact, is the date of the birth of Yeshua. This is done by establishing several things:

1)The date that Gabriel the angel tells Zechariah, the soon to be father of Yochanan, about his son's birth. (The birthdate of Yochanan (John) is established by going forward nine months, the term of pregnancy).

2)The approximate date of Miriam's (Mary's) conception.

3)The date of Herod's death.

The date that Gabriel the angel told Zechariah that he and his wife were going to have Yochanan is established from the following. Luke 1.5 states that Zechariah is a priest of the course of Abijah. King David, according to I Chronicles twenty-four, had divided the priestly families into twenty-four groups. Each group was called a course, and named after the head of that particular family. Each course served for one week in the first half of the year, and for another week the second half of the year. This was in addition to the weeks of Hag haMatzah, Shavuot, and Sukkot, when all the courses were required to be present (Deuteronomy 16.16). Therefore, the first course served the first week of the year (Aviv); the second course, the second week; then all the courses, the third, because it was Hag haMatzah, and so on. I Chronicles 24.10 lists the course of Abijah as the eighth course. This course would serve the tenth week of the first half of the year, having allowed two weeks for Hag haMatzah and Shavuot. It is at this time that Zechariah receives the prophecy of Yochanan's birth.

> And it came to pass, that, while he executed the priest's office before G-d in the order of his course, according to the custom of the priest's office, his lot was to burn incense when he went into the Temple of the L-rd. And the whole multitude of the people were praying without at the time of incense. And there appeared unto him an angel of the L-rd standing on the right side of the altar of incense. And when Zechariah saw him, he was troubled, and fear fell upon him. But the angel said unto him, Fear not Zechariah: for thy prayer is heard; and thy wife Elizabeth shall bear thee a son, and thou shalt call his name Yochanan.
>
> Luke 1.8-13

Due to the laws of separation (Leviticus 12.5;15.19,25), two additional weeks have to be counted. Allowing for this and going forward a normal pregnancy, the time of Yochanan's birth (if this is the first half of the year) would be approximately Pesach, when it is expected that Elijah will appear.

Six months following Elizabeth's conception, the angel Gabriel is sent to Miriam (Mary), the cousin of Elizabeth.

> And in the sixth month the angel Gabriel was sent from G-d unto a city of Galilee, named Nazareth, to a virgin espoused to a man whose name was Joseph, of the house of David; and the virgin's name was Miriam (Mary). And the angel came in unto her, and said, Hail, thou that art highly favoured, the L-rd is with thee: blessed art thou among women. And when she saw him, she was troubled at his saying, and cast in her mind what manner of salutation this should be. And the angel said unto her, Fear not, Miriam (Mary): for thou hast found favour with G-d. And, behold, thou shalt conceive in thy womb, and bring forth a son, and shalt call His name Yeshua. He shall be great, and shall be called the

Son of the Highest; and the L-rd G-d shall give unto Him the
throne of His father David: And He shall reign over the house of
Jacob for ever; and of His kingdom there shall be no end.
Luke 1.26-33

Starting at Chanukkah, which begins on Kislev 25 and
continues for eight days, and counting through the nine months
of Miriam's pregnancy brings one to the approximate time of
Sukkot.

The question arises, "How can it be known that Zechariah
was given the prophecy about Yochanan in the first half of the
year rather than the last? The key is found in the life and death
of King Herod. Herod, a man hated by the Jewish people, figures
prominently into the birth of Yeshua. In Mattatiyahu (Matthew)
two he is visited by "wise men from the East."

Now when Yeshua was born in Bethlehem of Judea in the days
of Herod the king, behold, there came wise men from the east
to Jerusalem, saying, Where is He that is born King of the Jews?
for we have seen His star in the east, and are come to worship
Him.
Mattatiyahu (Matthew) 2.1-2

From the information in this passage, it can be understood
that the "wise men" are Jewish. While the verse does not tell how
many wise men there are, it does give reference to where they
were from. In the Bible, the "land of the East" is always the land
of Babylon (see Genesis 29.1; Judges 6.3). During the first century
C.E., the largest Jewish population was in Babylon. These people
were the descendants of the captivity of Nebuchadnezzar. Even
though Ezra, Nehemiah, and others had returned, most of the
people had remained behind. The fact that the wise men are
looking for the Jewish messiah, who was only expected by the
Jewish people, should be noted. A prophecy relating to the
Messiah that only the Jewish people were aware of is found in the
book of Numbers.

The Birth of Yeshua During Sukkot   **167**

> I shall see Him, but not now: I shall behold Him, but not nigh: there shall come a Star out of Jacob, and a Sceptre shall rise out of Israel, and shall smite the corners of Moab, and destroy all the children of Sheth.
>
> Numbers 24.17

Because of the prophecy, a star was related to the coming of the Messiah. An example of this is seen when, about one hundred years after the time of Yeshua, Rabbi Akiva mistakenly proclaimed a military leader to be the Messiah. He was titled "Bar Kochba," which means "Son of the Star."

The rabbis or the sages were known as the "chakamim," which means "the wise men." The sage Daniel was referred to by this same title. A related word, "mag" is also used for "wise men." The Greek "magi" is taken from the Babylonian word "mag," which has a number of meanings. It is true that the word does mean "astrologer;" however, this is not its only usage. The same word is used for scientist, counselor, or scholar. It is an obvious conclusion, then, that the Jewish sages or wise men from Babylon, knowing the prophecy of Numbers 24.17, relating it correctly to the Messiah, and having seen His star, traveled to Jerusalem to do homage.

Herod was possibly one of the coldest and most bloodthirsty men who ever lived. He killed his sons, his favorite wife, and thousands of innocent people. His fear of losing his throne drove him to insanity. Augustus Caesar, having noted that Herod observed Jewish Law and therefore would not eat pork, once made the statement that it was better to be a pig in the house of Herod than to be one of his sons. It is no surprise that Herod sought the child's life, nor that all of Jerusalem would be troubled as Herod received this news.

> When Herod the king had heard these things, he was troubled, and all Jerusalem with him.
>
> Mattatiyahu (Matthew) 2.3

Traditional teaching is that the "wise men" appeared about a year to eighteen months after the birth of Yeshua. This has been based upon Herod's killing of the male children under two years, according to the date that the wise men had given him for the appearance of the star.

> Then Herod, when he had privily called the wise men, inquired of them diligently what time the star appeared. And he sent them to Bethlehem, and said, Go and search diligently for the young child; and when ye have found him, bring me word again, that I may come and worship him also. Then Herod, when he saw that he was mocked of the wise men, was exceeding wroth, and sent forth, and slew all the children that were in Bethlehem, and in all the coasts thereof, from two years old and under, according to the time which he had diligently inquired of the wise men.
>
> Mattatiyahu (Matthew) 2.7-8,16

It was the custom in ancient Israel to count the years of one's age from the date of conception; therefore, Herod actually killed the children one year old and under according to the way that age is calculated today. In fact, the wise men arrive in Jerusalem either just prior to or at the time of Yeshua's birth.

It is important to note that up to this time, no one in Jerusalem, including the Temple priest, had heard that Yeshua had been born. Knowing the nature of Herod, and his practice of having spies throughout the countryside, it is impossible that he would not have heard of his birth. Luke's account of the birth relates the experience of the shepherds of Bethlehem, who after seeing the newborn Yeshua, broadcast what they have seen and heard to the entire region.

The Birth of Yeshua During Sukkot   **169**

> And when they had seen it, they made known abroad the saying
> which was told them concerning this child.
>
> Luke 2.17

Realizing that Bethlehem is within five miles of Jerusalem makes it very improbable that Herod or the Temple priest would be ignorant of His birth. Further proof is seen in that forty days after the birth of Yeshua, Miriam (Mary) carries Yeshua to the Temple for her purification and His dedication. It is here that two well known individuals within the Temple compound and make known prophesy concerning the child.

And when the days of her purification according to the law of Moses were accomplished, they brought him to Jerusalem, to present him to the L-rd; (As it is written in the law of the L-rd, Every male that openeth the womb shall be called holy to the L-rd;) And to offer a sacrifice according to that which is said in the law of the L-rd, A pair of turtledoves, or two young pigeons. And, behold, there was a man in Jerusalem, whose name was Simeon; and the same man was just and devout, waiting for the consolation of Israel: and the Ruach haKodesh (the Holy Spirit) was upon him. And it was revealed unto him by the Ruach haKodesh, that he should not see death, before he had seen the L-rd's Messiah. And he came by the Spirit into the temple: and when the parents brought in the child Yeshua, to do for him after the custom of the law, Then took he him up in his arms, and blessed G-d, and said, L-rd, now lettest thou thy servant depart in peace, according to thy word: For mine eyes have seen thy salvation, Which thou hast prepared before the face of all people; A light to lighten the Gentiles, and the glory of thy people Israel. And Joseph and his mother marvelled at those things which were spoken of him. And Simeon blessed them, and said unto Miriam his mother, Behold, this child is set for the fall and rising again of many in Israel; and for a sign which shall be spoken against; (Yea, a sword shall pierce through thy own soul also,) that the thoughts of many hearts may be revealed. And there was one Anna, a prophetess, the daughter of Phanuel, of the tribe of Asher: she was of a great age, and had lived with a husband

seven years from her virginity; And she was a widow of about fourscore and four years, which departed not from the temple, but served G-d with fastings and prayers night and day. And she coming in that instant gave thanks likwise unto the L-rd, and spake of him to all them that looked for redemption in Jerusalem.
Luke 2.22-38

Having realized that it is impossible for the wise men to arrive after these events, it can be assumed that they must have spoken to Herod about the time of His birth. Traveling on to Bethlehem, they found the child and His parents in a house, (Mattatityahu 2.11); whereas, in the Luke account the shepherds found Him in a stable (Luke 2.7,16). There is no discrepancy between these two accounts, for likely the new mother and child were moved from the stable following the birth. The fact that He was born in a stable is a clue to the time of His birth, for in Hebrew a stable is called a "sukkah" (Genesis 33.17). "Sukkot," the name of the festival, is the plural form of this word. It is even significant that they had to seek cover in the "sukkah" due to "no room in the inn" (Luke 2.7). It was only during the three pilgrim festivals (Pesach, Hag haMatzah, and Shavuot) that Bethlehem would overflow with people. The thousands of pilgrims coming to Jerusalem for the festivals would spill over to the surrounding towns. In ancient times, reporting for a census would be done over a several month period due to the difficulties of travel, as well as the economics of an agricultural society. It is highly improbable that so many people would be in Bethlehem for Caesar's census all at one time.

As stated above, Joseph and Miriam (Mary) bring the child into Jerusalem forty days after Yeshua's birth. This indicates that Herod died within this same forty days. The chronology of these forty days is imperative in correctly finding His birth date. The probable scenario is this: Joseph and Miriam (Mary) come to Jerusalem for the festival of Sukkot (September or October), planning to stay in the nearby Bethlehem in order to register for the census. Unable to find a room at the inn, they are given shelter in a stable, which just happens to be a Sukkah. During the night the wise men arrive in Jerusalem and speak to Herod. Meanwhile, Miriam gives birth. The heavenly host appear to the shepherds, proclaiming that the Messiah has been born. They go to pay Him homage in the stable, while the wise men are making their way to Bethlehem. The shepherds leave to "noise it abroad," and Miriam is moved to a house. The wise men arrive and during the night are warned by G-d concerning Herod. Joseph and Miriam take the child and flee to Egypt and remain there until they are told by G-d that Herod is dead. On returning to Judea, they dedicate Yeshua according to the Law, receiving the prophecies of Anna and Simeon. After this, they turn aside into Galilee, where they will live.

It is apparent that as long as Herod was alive, they could not appear at the Temple. Therefore, if the approximate date of Herod's death could be determined, it would establish the season of Yeshua's birth. The Jewish historian, Josephus, who lived during the first century C.E., documents in detail Herod's death.

Josephus relates that Herod became very ill immediately following an act of impiety against the priesthood, at which time an eclipse of the moon occurred. This eclipse, the only one mentioned by Josephus, happened March 13 in the year of the Julian period 4710, and the fourth year before the Common Era. Herod's illness lasted several months and is documented in great detail as being painful and distressful. Many times cures were sought and brought about temporary relief; however, nothing prevented imminent death. According to Josephus' calculations, Herod's death occurred about September, in the fourth year before the Common Era. Therefore, with the knowledge that

Herod died in autumn, the same time of year as Sukkot, and that his death was within forty days of the birth of Yeshua, it is established that Yeshua was born at this time of year.

The Birth of Yeshua During Sukkot

APPENDIX II

TITLES OF THE DAY OF THE L-RD

1. **The Day of the L-rd of Hosts**
   Isaiah 2.12

2. **The Day of Punishment (Visitation)**
   Isaiah 10.3

3. **The Day of the L-rd**

Isaiah 13.6	*Amos 5.18*
Ezekiel 13.5	*Amos 5.20*
Ezekiel 30.3	*Zephaniah 1.7*
Joel 1.15	*Zephaniah 1.14*
Joel 2.1	*Zechariah 14.1*
Joel 2.11	*I Thessalonians 5.2*
Joel 3.14	*II Peter 3.10*

4. **The Day of His Fierce Anger**

Isaiah 13.13	*Lamentations 1.12*

5. **The Day of The L-rd Gives You Rest**
   Isaiah 14.3

6. **The Day of Grief and Desperate Sorrow**
   Isaiah 17.11

7. **A Day of Trouble**

Isaiah 22.5	*Ezekiel 7.7*

8. The Day of The East Wind
Isaiah 27.8

9. The Day of The Great Slaughter
Isaiah 30.25

10. The Day of The L-rd's Vengeance
Isaiah 34.8

11. A Day of Trouble and Rebuke and Blasphemy
Isaiah 37.3   *II Kings 19.3*

12. The Day of Salvation
Isaiah 49.8

13. The Day of Vengeance of Our G-d
Isaiah 61.2

14. The Day of Vengeance
Isaiah 63.4   *Proverbs 6.34*

15. The Day of Slaughter
Jeremiah 12.3

16. The Day of Affliction
Jeremiah 16.19

17. The Day of Doom
Jeremiah 17.17 (evil)
Jeremiah 17.18 (evil)
Jeremiah 51.2 (trouble)
Amos 6.3 (evil)

Job 21.30 (destruction)

18. The Day of Their Calamity
Jeremiah 18.17
Jeremiah 46.21
Deuteronomy 32.35

19. The Day of the L-rd G-d of Hosts
Jeremiah 46.10

20. A Day of Vengeance
Jeremiah 46.10

21. The Day You Have Announced
Lamentations 1.21

22. The Day of His Anger
Lamentations 2.1

23. The Day We Have Waited For
Lamentations 2.16

24. The Day of Your Anger
Lamentations 2.21

25. The Day of The L-rd's Anger
Lamentations 2.22
Zephaniah 2.2
Zephaniah 2.3

26. Behold, The Day
Ezekiel 7.10

27.The Day of The Wrath of The L-rd
Ezekiel 7.19

28.The Day
Ezekiel 30.2
Ezekiel 30.3
Joel 1.15
Malachi 4.1
I Corinthians 3.13

29.A Day of Clouds
Ezekiel 30.3

30.The Day of Egypt
Ezekiel 30.9

31.The Day of Your Fall
Ezekiel 32.10

32.The Day That I Am Glorified
Ezekiel 39.13

33.The Day of Jezreel
Hosea 1.11

34.The Day of Rebuke
Hosea 5.9

35.The Day of Our King
Hosea 7.5

36. The Appointed Day
Hosea 9.5

37. The Day of The Feast of The L-rd
Hosea 9.5

38. The Days of Punishment
Hosea 9.7

39. The Days of Recompense
Hosea 9.7

40. The Day of Darkness and Gloominess
Joel 2.2
Zephaniah 1.15

41. A Day of Clouds and Thick Darkness
Joel 2.2
Zephaniah 1.15

42. The Great and Terrible Day of The L-rd
Joel 2.31

43. The Day of Battle
Amos 1.14
Zechariah 14.3
Psalms 140.7
Proverbs 21.31

44. The Day of The Whirlwind
Amos 1.14

Titles of the Day of the L-rd   **179**

45. The Day of The L-rd Upon All Nations
Obadiah 15

46. The Day of Your Watchman and Your Punishment
Micah 7.4

47. The Day of Trouble
Nahum 1.7
Habakkuk 3.16
Psalms 50.15

48. The Day of Jacob's Trouble
Jeremiah 30.7

49. The Day of His Preparation
Nahum 2.3

50. The Day of The L-rd's Sacrifice
Zephaniah 1.8

51. The Great Day of The L-rd
Zephaniah 1.14

52. A Day of Wrath
Zephaniah 1.15

53. A Day of Trouble and Distress
Zephaniah 1.15

54. A Day of Devastation and Desolution
Zephaniah 1.15

55.A Day of Trumpet and Alarm
Zephaniah 1.16

56.The Day of The L-rd's Wrath
Zephaniah 1.18

57.The Day of His Coming
Malachi 3.2

58.The Great and Dreadful Day of The L-rd
Malachi 4.5

59.The Day of Judgement
Matthew 10.15   *Mark 6.11*
Matthew 11.24   *II Peter 2.9*
Matthew 12.36   *I John 4.17*

60.The Son of Man Will Be in His Day
Luke 17.24

61.The Day When the Son of Man is Revealed
Luke 17.30

62.The Great and Notable Day of The L-rd
Acts 2.20

63.The Day of Wrath and Revelation of The Righteous Judgement of G-d
Romans 2.5

64.The Day of Our L-rd Yeshua HaMaschiach
I Corinthians 1.8

65. The Day of The L-rd Yeshua
II Corinthians 1.14

66. The Day of Redemption
Ephesians 4.30

67. The Day of Messiah
Philippians 1.10
Philippians 2.16

68. The Day of Yeshua haMaschiach
Philippians 1.6

69. The Day of Judgement and Perdition of UnG-dly Men
II Peter 3.7

70. The Day of G-d
II Peter 3.12

71. The Judgement of The Great Day
Jude 6

72. The Great Day of His Wrath
Revelation 6.17

73. The Great Day of G-d Almighty
Revelation 16.14

74. The Day of My Calamity
II Samuel 22.19

75. The Day of His Wrath
Job 20.28
Psalms 110.5

76. The Day of Wrath
Job 21.30
Proverbs 11.4

77. The Day of Battle and War
Job 38.23

78. The Day of My Trouble
Psalms 77.2
Psalms 86.7
Psalms 102.2

79. The Day of Your Power
Psalms 110.3

80. The Day of Adversity
Proverbs 24.10

81. The Day When the Keepers of the House Tremble
Ecclesiastes 12.3

82. The Day of His Espousals
Song of Solomon 3.11

83. The Day of The Gladness of His Heart
Song of Solomon 3.11

84.A Day on Which He Will Judge the World in Righteousness by Whom He Had Ordained

Acts 17.31

85.The Day the L-rd Binds Up the Bruise of His People

Isaiah 30.26 (days)

THE DAY OF TROUBLE - SYNONYMS

TROUBLE	*II Kings 19.3*
	I Chronicles 22.14
	II Chronicles 15.4; 29.8; 32.18
	Nehemiah 9.27,32
	Job 3.26; 38.23
	Psalms 9.9,13; 10.1; 13.4; 20.1; 22.11; 25.17,22; 27.5; 31.7,9; 34.6,17; 37.39; 41.1; 46.1; 50.15; 54.7; 59.16; 60.11; 66.14; 69.17; 71.20; 73.5; 77.2; 78.33,49; 81.7; 83.17; 86.7; 88.3; 90.7; 91.7; 102.2; 104.29; 107.6,19,26,28; 108.12; 116.3; 119.143; 138.7; 142.2; 143.11
	Proverbs 11.8; 12.13; 25.19
	Isaiah 8.22; 22.5; 26.16; 30.6; 32.10,11; 33.2; 37.3; 46.7; 57.20; 65.16,23
	Jeremiah 2.27,28; 8.15; 11.12,14; 14.8,19; 30.7; 51.2
	Lamentations 1.21
	Ezekiel 7.7,27; 26.18; 27.35; 32.13
	Daniel 12.1

Nahum 1.7

Habakkuk 3.16

Zephaniah 1.15

INDIGNATION *Deuteronomy 29.28;*

Job 10.17

Psalms 69.24; 78.49; 102.10

Isaiah 10.5,25; 13.5; 26.20; 30.27,30; 34.2; 66.14

Jeremiah 10.10; 15.17; 50.25

Lamentations 2.6

Ezekiel 21.31; 22.24,31

Daniel 8.19; 11.36

Micah 7.9

Nahum 1.6

Habakkuk 3.12

Zephaniah 3.8

Malachi 1.4

Hebrews 10.27

Revelations 14.10

TRAVAIL *Genesis 3.16; 35.16-20; 38.27-28; 48.3*

II Kings 19.3

Psalms 48.3-6

Isaiah 13.8; 21.3; 23.4; 26.17;37.3; 42.14; 54.1; 66.7-9

Jeremiah 4.31; 6.24; 13.21; 22.23; 30.6; 31.8; 48.41; 49.22-24; 50.43

Hosea 9.11-12; 13.13

Micah 4.9-10; 5.3

Matthew 24.8

Mark 13.8

John 16.21-24

I Thessalonians 5.3

Revelation 12.2

WHIRLWIND *II Kings 2.1,11*

Job 37.9; 38.1; 40.6

Psalms 58.9

Proverbs 1.27; 10.25

Isaiah 5.28; 17.13; 40.24; 41.16; 66.15

Jeremiah 4.13; 23.19; 25.32; 30.23

Ezekiel 1.4

Daniel 11.40

Hosea 8.7; 13.3

Amos 1.14

Nahum 1.3

Habakkuk 3.14

Zechariah 7.14

Synonyms for the Day of Trouble

Bibliography

Adler, Herbert M. and others. *Service of the Synagogue: New Year and Atonement.* New York: Hebrew Publishing Company.

Agnon, S. Y. *Days of Awe.* New York: Schocken Books, 1965.

Birnbaum, Philip. *High Holyday Prayer Book.* New York: Hebrew Publishing Company, 1951.

Blackman, Philip. *Mishnayoth,* vol. 1-7. New York: The Judaica Press, Ltd., 1983.

Bloch, Abraham P. *The Biblical and Historical Background of the Jewish Holy Days.* New York: KTAV Publishing House, Inc., 1978.

Bonsirven, Joseph. *Palestinian Judaism in the Time of Jesus Christ.* New York: Holt, Rinehart and Winston.

Braude, William G. *The Midrash on Psalms.* New Haven: Yale University Press, 1959.

de Vaux, Roland. *Ancient Israel,* Vol. 1-2. New York: McGraw-Hill Book Company, 1965.

Doukhan, Jacques. *Drinking at the Sources.* Mountain View: Pacific Press Publishing Association, 1981.

Edersheim, Alfred. *Sketches of Jewish Social Life in the Days of Christ.* Grand Rapids: Wm. B. Eerdmans Publishing Company, 1982.

The Temple. Grand Rapids: Wm. B. Eerdmans Publishing Company, 1980.

Feuer, Rabbi Avrohom Chaim. *Tehillim.* Brooklyn: Mesorah Publications, Ltd., 1979.

Foote-Moore, George. *Judaism in the First Centuries of the Christian Era,* Vol. 1-2. Cambridge: Harvard University Press, 1927.

Gaster, Theodor H. *Festivals of the Jewish Year.* New York: Morrow Quill Paperbacks, 1978.

Gianotti, Charles R. *The New Testament and the Mishnah.* Grand Rapids: Baker Book House, 1983.

Goodman, Philip. *The Passover Anthology.* Philadelphia: The Jewish Publication Society of America, 1961.

The Rosh Hashanah Anthology. Philadelphia: The Jewish Publication Society of America, 1973.

The Shavuot Anthology. Philadelphia: The Jewish Publication Society of America, 1974.

The Sukkot and Simhat Torah Anthology. Philadelphia: The Jewish Publication Society of America, 1973.

The Yom Kippur Anthology. Philadelphia: The Jewish Publication Society of America, 1983.

Hertz, Dr. Joseph H. *Daily Prayer Book.* New York: Bloch Publishing Company, 1963.

The Pentateuch and Haftorahs. London: Soncino Press, 1958.

Jastrow, Marcus. *Dictionary of the Targumim, Talmud Babli, Yerushalmi, and Midrashic Literature.* New York: The Judaica Press, Inc., 1985.

Kac, Arthur W. *The Messianic Hope.* Grand Rapids: Baker Book House, 1975.

Kaplan, Rabbi Aryeh. *Made in Heaven, A Jewish Wedding Guide.* New York: Moznaim Publishing Corporation, 1983.

Kaplan, Rabbi Aryeh, Ed. *Me'am Lo'es - The Torah Anthology.* New York: Maznaim Publishing Corporation, 1979.

Kieval, Herman. *The High Holy Days.* New York: The Burning Bush Press, 1959.

Lascelle, Ruth Specter. *The Passover Feast.* Seattle: Bedrock Press, 1975.

Neusner, Jacob. *The Oral Torah - The Sacred Books of Judaism, and Introduction.* San Francisco: Harper and Row Publishers, 1986.

Price, Walter K. *Next Year in Jerusalem.* Chicago: Moody Press, 1975.

Rosenberg, Rabbi A. J. *Isaiah - A New English Translation*, Vol. 1-2. New York: The Judaica Press Inc., 1982.

Rotberg, Rabbi Tzvi. *Rosh Hashana - The Akeida.* New York: Moznaim Publishing Corporation, 1983.

Safrai, S., and M. Stern, Ed. in cooperation with D. Flusser and W. C. van Unnik. *The Jewish People in the First Century*, Vol. 1-2. Philadelphia: Fortress Press, 1974.

Schauss, Hayyim. *The Jewish Festivals From Their Beginnings to Our Own Day.* New York: Union of American Hebrew Congregations, 1938.

Scherman, Rabbi Nosson and Rabbi Meir Zlotowitz, Ed. *Artscroll Mishnah Series.* Brooklyn: Mesorah Publications, Ltd., 1983.

History of the Jewish People, the Second Temple Era. Brooklyn: Mesorah Publication, Ltd., 1982.

Rosh Hashanah - Its Significance, Laws, and Prayers. Brooklyn: Mesorah Publications, Ltd., 1983.

Shir HaShirim - Song of Songs. Brooklyn: Mesorah Publications, Ltd., 1979.

Succos - Its Significance, Laws, and Prayers. Brooklyn: Mesorah Publications, Ltd., 1982.

Tehillim - A New Translation with a Commentary Anthologized from Talmudic, Midrashic and Rabbinic Sources. Brooklyn: Mesorah Publications, Ltd., 1978.

Scholem, Gershom. *The Messianic Idea in Judaism.* New York: Schocken Books, 1971.

Silverman, Rabbi Morris. *High Holiday Prayer Book.* Hartford: Prayer Book Press Publishers, 1951.

Strassfeld, Michael. *The Jewish Holidays - A Guide and Commentary.* New York: Harper and Row Publishers, 1985.

Vermes, Geza. *Jesus the Jew - A Historian's Reading of the Gospels.* New York: Macmillan Publishing Co., Inc., 1974.

Waskow, Arthur. *Seasons of Our Joy.* New York: Bantam Books, 1982.

Weissman, Rabbi Moshe. *The Midrash Says, Vol. 1-5.* Brooklyn: Benei Yakov Publications, 1980.

Werblowsky, R. J. Zwi and Geoffrey Wigoder, Ed. *The Encyclopedia of the Jewish Religion.* New York: Adama Books, 1986.

Whiston, William, translator. *Josephus Complete Works.* Grand Rapids: Kregel Publications, 1978.

Yellin, Burt. *Messiah: a Rabbinic and Scriptural Viewpoint.* Denver: Congregation Roeh Israel, 1984.

Zakon, Miriam Stark, Ed. *Tz'enah Ur'enah - The Classic Anthology of Torah Lore and Midrashic Comment.* Brooklyn: Mesorah Publications, Ltd., 1983.

Bibliography

Glossary

Afikomen	*Greek word meaning that which comes after. It is represented in a broken piece of matzah wrapped in linen and buried (hidden).*
Akeida	*The binding of the sacrifice.*
Asham	*A guilt offering made by one who has sinned against his fellow man.*
Athid Lavo	*The coming age.*
Atzeret	*A festive gathering for the conclusion of a festive season, a concluding feast.*
Basar	*Good news (same as gospel).*
Beit Hamikdash	*The sanctuary or Temple in Jerusalem.*
Beit haShoevah	*The House of the Waterpouring.*
C.E.	*Common Era (same as A.D.).*
Chupah	*Canopy which represents the honeymoon chamber.*
Cohan haGadol	*The High Priest.*
Gan Eden	*The Garden of Eden.*
Go'el	*Redeemer.*
Hag haMatzah	*Festival of Unleavened Bread.*
HaSatan	*The Adversary (same as Satan).*
Hataat	*A sin offering made by one who has sinned against G-d.*
Hatikva	*The hope.*
High Holy Days	*A ten day period from Rosh haShanah to Yom Kippur.*
Kedushin	*The wedding ceremony.*
Ketubah	*A second marriage contract.*

Malkut Shamayim	*The Kingdom of Heaven.*
Mashiach	*Anointed one (same as Messiah or Christ).*
Matan Torah	*The giving of the law or instruction.*
Mattitiyahu	*Hebrew name for Matthew.*
Matzah	*Unleavened bread.*
Mayim Hayim	*Living water.*
Mikrah	*Convocation, a rehearsal or recital.*
Mo'ed	*set time or appointed time.*
Mussaf	*Additional service for Sabbath and festivals.*
Natzal	*Deliverance, used to denote the rapture.*
Neilah	*Closing of the gate (part of the service of Yom Kippur).*
Nevi'im	*The Prophets.*
Olam Haba	*The World to Come.*
Oseif	*Gathering of the nobles.*
Pesach	*Passover.*
Proselyte	*Convert to Judaism.*
Ramah	*Seat of Idolatry.*
Rashim	*The wholly wicked.*
Rav Shaul	*Rabbi Paul (the Apostle Paul).*
Rosh haShanah	*Head of the year, Jewish New Year.*
Ruach HaKodesh	*The Holy Spirit.*
Seder	*The Passover meal, order.*
Selichot	*Penitential prayers.*
Shabbaton	*Seven high Sabbaths.*
Shacharit	*Morning Service.*
Shavuot	*The Day of Pentecost, receiving of the Torah, and the beginning of the wheat harvest. Also, it represents the betrothal between Israel and the L-rd.*

Shemini Atzeret	*The day following Sukkot and the end of that festival.*
Shitre Erusin	*A betrothal contract.*
Shofar	*Trumpet made from a ram's horn.*
Shofar haGadol	*The Great Trumpet.*
Sukkah	*Booth, Covering.*
Sukkot	*The Feast of Tabernacles or Booths.*
Tanach	*The Hebrew Bible.*
Teruah	*An awakening blast.*
Teshuvah	*Repentance from sin, spiritual reawakening. A desire to strengthen the connection between oneself and the sacred.*
Torah	*Instruction (teaching) or law.*
Tzaddikim	*Saints or the Righteous.*
Yamin Nora'im	*The Days of Awe.*
Yeshua	*Hebrew name meaning salvation (same as Jesus).*
Yitzhak	*Hebrew name for Isaac.*
Yochanan	*Hebrew name for John.*
Yom haDin	*The Day of Judgement.*
Yom haPeduth	*The Day of Redemption.*
Yom haZikkaron	*The Day of Remembrance.*
Yom Kippur	*The Day of Atonement.*
Yom Teruah	*The Feast of Trumpets.*
Zikkaron	*A Memorial.*
Zikhrnot	*A portion of the Rosh HaShanah service that deals with divine remembrance.*